| DATE DUE | | | |
|---|---|---|---|
| | | | |
| | | | |
| | | | |
| | | | |
| | | | |
| | | | |
| | | | |
| | | | |
| | | | |
| | | | |
| | | | |
| | | | |
| | | | |

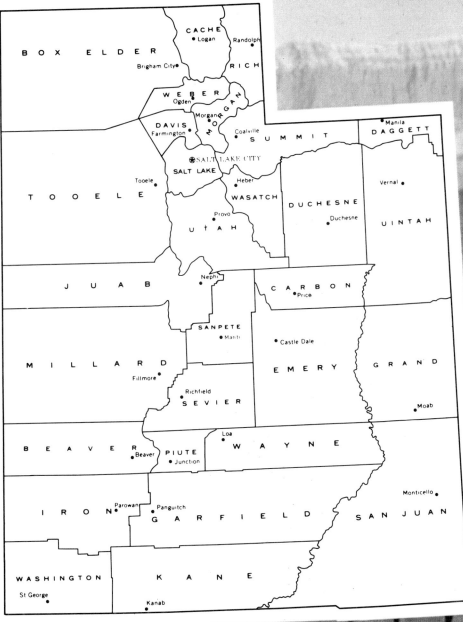

CACHE
Logan
Randolph
BOX ELDER
Brigham City
RICH
WEBER
Ogden
MORGAN
Morgan
DAVIS
Farmington
Coalville
SUMMIT
DAGGETT
Manila
SALT LAKE CITY
SALT LAKE
Tooele
Heber
Vernal
WASATCH
DUCHESNE
TOOELE
Provo
Duchesne
UINTAH
UTAH
Nephi
JUAB
CARBON
Price
SANPETE
Manti
Castle Dale
MILLARD
EMERY
GRAND
Fillmore
Richfield
Moab
SEVIER
Loa
BEAVER
PIUTE
WAYNE
Beaver
Junction
Monticello
Parowan
IRON
Panguitch
GARFIELD
SAN JUAN
WASHINGTON
KANE
St George
Kanab

The New

Enchantment of America

# UTAH

By Allan Carpenter

 CHILDRENS PRESS, CHICAGO

# ACKNOWLEDGMENTS

**For assistance in the preparation of the revised edition, the author thanks:**
CLAUDIA HAMEDA MUELLER and WILLIAM SPIGEL, Utah Travel Council, and WILLIAM CARPENTER, Librarian, The Church of Jesus Christ of Latter-Day Saints.

*American Airlines*—Anne Vitaliano, Director of Public Relations; *Capitol Historical Society,* Washington, D. C.; *Newberry Library,* Chicago, Dr. Lawrence Towner, Director; *Northwestern University Library,* Evanston, Illinois; *United Airlines*—John P. Grember, Manager of Special Promotions; Joseph P. Hopkins, Manager, News Bureau; Carl Provorse, *Carpenter Publishing House.*

UNITED STATES GOVERNMENT AGENCIES: *Department of Agriculture*—Robert Hailstock, Jr., Photography Division, Office of Communication; Donald C. Schuhart, Information Division, Soil Conservation Service. *Army*—Doran Topolosky, Public Affairs Office, Chief of Engineers, Corps of Engineers. *Department of Interior*—Louis Churchville, Director of Communications; EROS Space Program—Phillis Wiepking, Community Affairs; Charles Withington, Geologist; Mrs. Ruth Herbert, Information Specialist; Bureau of Reclamation; National Park Service—Fred Bell and the individual sites; Fish and Wildlife Service—Bob Hines, Public Affairs Office. *Library of Congress*—Dr. Alan Fern, Director of the Department of Research; Sara Wallace, Director of Publications; Dr. Walter W. Ristow, Chief, Geography and Map Division; Herbert Sandborn, Exhibits Officer. *National Archives*—Dr. James B. Rhoads, Archivist of the United States; Albert Meisel, Assistant Archivist for Educational Programs; David Eggenberger, Publications Director; Bill Leary, Still Picture Reference; James Moore, Audio-Visual Archives. *United States Postal Service*—Herb Harris, Stamps Division.

**For assistance in the preparation of the first edition, the author thanks:**
Consultants James M. Oswald, Secondary Supervisor, Social Studies, Salt Lake City Public School District and Eva May Green, Elementary Supervisor, Social Studies, Salt Lake City Public School District; Calvin L. Rampton, Governor; James D. Cannon, Director, Utah State Department of Tourism and Publicity; Harold S. Crane; Karol Hall; Joseph Fielding Smith, Historian, The Church of Jesus Christ of Latter-Day Saints; and Floretta Soltow.

**Illustrations on the preceding pages:**
Cover photograph: Mormon Temple, American Airlines
Page 1: Commemorative stamps of historic interest
Pages 2-3: Cowboys with cattle, USDA, Robert Hailstock, Jr.
Page 3: (Map) USDI Geological Survey
Pages 4-5: Salt Lake City area, EROS Space Photo, USDI Geological Survey, EROS Data Center

Project Editor, Revised Edition:
Joan Downing
Assistant Editor, Revised Edition:
Mary Reidy

**Library of Congress Cataloging in Publication Data**
Carpenter, John Allan, 1917-
Utah.
(His the new enchantment of America)
Includes index.
SUMMARY: A history of the state and a description of its mineral treasures, people, connection with Mormonism, and scenic attractions.
1. Utah—Juvenile literature.
[1. Utah] I. Title. II. Series.
F826.3.C3 1979 979.2 79-12433
ISBN 0-516-04144-4

# Contents

# A True Story to Set the Scene

"Whenever I waked I turned and gazed at the loom of the mighty arch against the clear night sky."

The man who wrote those words was one of the best-known men in American history, who had spread his sleeping bag on the rocks beneath the arch of the little-known Rainbow Bridge. The great man had traveled across the desert for days in order to experience the wonder of one of nature's greatest marvels.

He was Theodore Roosevelt—former president of the United States—rancher, big game hunter, statesman, Nobel Peace Prize winner, author, and as in this case, explorer and adventurer. To reach their destination in southern Utah, the Roosevelt party had traveled for five wearying days. A heaven-bursting storm interrupted their plodding journey through hot dusty wastes, past cliffs and boulders. They met Navajo shepherds and their flocks and waved at hogans, homes of the Navajo.

Finally, after the hardest part of the trip, they turned a corner and feasted their eyes on the spectacle they had come so far to see—the great Rainbow Bridge.

Here was a scene that would be celebrated in story and song if it were in Europe, but among the wonders of Utah it was then, as the former president said, "only one among many others, all equally unknown."

Rainbow Bridge had been discovered only the year after Roosevelt left the presidency. A year later, in 1910, President Taft had made it a National Monument. In 1913, after losing a bid for the presidency and after recovering from an attempted assassination, Roosevelt made this trip.

For a long time Roosevelt and his party stood silently looking at what he called "A triumphal arch rather than a bridge ... [it] spans the torrent bed in a majesty never shared by any arch ever reared by the mightiest conquerors among the nations of mankind."

At this particular time of year a number of rainwater pools were

*Opposite: Rainbow Bridge*

*Rainbow Bridge was made a national monument in 1910.*

lying in the natural basins of the rocks. Floating on his back in one of the pools just under the arch itself, the former president took a luxurious bath while he gazed in awe at the marvel above him.

Later they built a roaring fire beside one of the enormous legs of the bridge. Flames lit up the brilliant colors of the rocks, while a hearty meal cooked over the fire. The men laughed and joked as the two Indians of the party sat silently by, listening intently to the "big chief." A large moon rose, framed by the stone arch, bathing the bright cliffs with a cold white light, revealing the many ferns and hanging plants growing under overhanging shelves of rock.

Roosevelt unrolled his sleeping bag on the rocks immediately beneath the mighty arch, where he could marvel at it every time his sleep was interrupted.

When he thought about it later, this man, who had seen so many of the world's spectacles, called Rainbow Bridge "one of the wonders of the world," a tribute that could be applied almost equally well to endless other places of enchantment in fantastic Utah.

10

# Lay of the Land

## "WONDERFUL, OUTRAGEOUS, MYSTERIOUS, STRANGE!"

The correspondent sat on a pile of rocks. He put both feet down carefully on the desert sands, then placed his two hands on the sands. In this way Ernie Pyle, one of America's best-loved journalists, took notice of the "four corners." In that position he was touching four states—Utah, Colorado, New Mexico, and Arizona. This is the only place in the country where four states come together at a corner point.

This is only one of the many distinctions of Utah. Descriptions of this "wonderful, outrageous, mysterious, and strange" land seem too exaggerated to believe. Yet no words can describe this landscape with its variety, color, grandeur, charm, and beauty.

More unusual natural attractions are concentrated within the boundaries of this one state than in any other similar area of the world. Many of these forms are unique in Utah.

Much of Utah is still little known and unmapped. Many of its physical attractions are world renowned, but there are so many hard-to-reach points of equal or greater interest that numbers of them have not been seen by visitors on guided tours. The largest unknown and generally unexplored region in the United States is the Kaiparowits Plateau, west of the Escalante River.

Mountains; deserts; salt flats; caves; incredible canyons and valleys; rocky formations so varied as to defy description; cliffs like gigantic fortresses; towering, soaring bridges carved from solid rock; foaming muddy rivers and crystal mountain streams or springs; a lake of salt, and clear blue lakes; forests; and blooming valleys—all are only a part of the unique variety of Utah.

## BEFORE THE TIME OF MAN

The gigantic forces of nature that made Utah what it is today have been at work since time began. The story is "written" in the rock walls of the canyons, where wind, sand, and water have cut through the various layers of time, down to rocks that were laid in place before there was life of any kind on earth.

At least four times the land has been thrust up from below and then each time worn away during eons. Ancient seas advanced and retreated over much of the area, and the icy hands of glaciers were felt there.

More recently, but still before the time of man, probably about fifty thousand years ago, a great lake covered much of what is now northern Utah, extending far into present-day Nevada. This has been given the name of Lake Bonneville. It existed for about twenty-five thousand years and varied in size during its life. At each stage of its development and disappearance, the lake left what is called a terrace; these were the boundaries outlining the edge of Lake Bonneville. Three distinct series of ledge-like terraces still remain as proof of a lake that no man ever saw. Most of the main cities of Utah have been built on the terraces of ancient Lake Bonneville.

Present-day Great Salt Lake and Little Salt Lake near Parowan are all that remain of that ancient lake. The lakes may be called "vestigial remains."

Utah is also one of the most important areas preserving the fossilized remains of ancient plants and animals. Utah has been called a "treasure chest of fossil remains."

*Artist Robert Thom imagines a prehistoric scene. © 1964 by Michigan Bell Telephone Company*

Some of the world's largest graveyards of those great reptiles, the dinosaurs, may be seen in such places as Dinosaur National Monument (shared with Colorado), and the Cleveland-Lloyd Dinosaur Quarry in Emery County. Near Standing Rocks in the Colorado River Canyon is an area bearing ancient crinoids and sea shells, showing how the prehistoric seas once flooded this now high and dry land. Fossils of musk oxen, horses, camels, deer, mammoths, and mountain sheep have all been found in Utah. In the fall of 1964, mammoth skeletons were found in the area north and west of Salt Lake City. It had been doubted that mammoths roamed this valley, but the find gave proof of their presence.

Excellent "stands" of petrified wood are found in Utah. Those of Circle Cliffs petrified forests form one of the most extensive deposits of petrified logs anywhere.

## REARING ROCKS AND GORGEOUS GULLIES

The unusual and interesting beauty of Utah's land is the result of nature's sculpture. The "artist" has worked for millions of years with tools of wind, sand, and water to create carved art in countless rock forms. Some of these stand out on comparatively flat land. Others result from the eating away of surrounding country to form fantastic canyons where harder rocks stand up in great, strange shapes.

There are two kinds of canyons in Utah: mountain canyons, where the valley has been cut through a mountain or mountain range, and eroded canyons, where a stream channel has simply widened and deepened. Big Cottonwood near Salt Lake City is a perfect example of a mountain canyon, and the Virgin River Canyon near St. George is an eroded type.

It has been said that everybody in Utah has his favorite canyon—the sylvan beauty of Logan Canyon, Cache Valley, eroded Snow Canyon, the canyons of the Escalante River, Maple Canyon, where boulders hang out at angles, clutched in natural cement, or the awesome majesty of Zion.

Of the wind and water "carvings," those of Monument Valley are probably the best-known examples. Spires of rock—some thin, some bulky—rise from the floor of this valley. Their brilliant colors of purples, reds, and oranges are not duplicated anywhere. The rock formations of Bryce could be studied for months or years and the visitor would still have much to see. Strangely, although Bryce has the word "canyon" in its name, it is not a true canyon. Instead, it is an escarpment.

Utah's natural bridges are among its most renowned natural wonders. No other area of Utah's size has so many natural bridges. The number is amazing. Bridges and arches are still being discovered or re-discovered. A National Geographic expedition as late as 1961 put several new ones on the map in the region where the Green and Colorado rivers join. It may be years before all the arches and natural bridges are listed.

The most famous and beautiful natural bridge in the world is Rainbow Bridge. It is also the largest known. The 278-foot (85-meter) Capitol dome at Washington, D.C., could be placed under this 309-foot (94-meter) natural arch. It takes its name from the Indian legend that a rainbow was turned to stone to permit hero gods to escape a flood. Natural Bridges National Monument and Capitol Reef National Monument both add to the variety and number of Utah's natural bridges.

Towers, needles, spires, cathedrals, goblins, book cliffs, standing rocks, sitting rocks, rearing rocks, and even seemingly leaping rocks dot the landscape in bewildering array and almost blinding color.


## WATERS: FLOWING AND STANDING

Even the rivers of Utah are unusual and distinctive. The San Juan, in one area, travels in a series of U-shaped curves. The technical name for these loops is "entrenched meander," but they are popularly called the Goosenecks of the San Juan. Here the river flows 6 miles (9.6 kilometers) to travel only 1 mile (1.6 kilometers), and it has carved its goosenecks almost 1,200 feet (365.8 meters)

*A float trip on the Green River.*

deep. This is called the "world's best example of an entrenched meander." The great bend of the San Juan travels 9 miles (14.5 kilometers) and comes back to only a half mile (.8 kilometers) from its starting point. Despite its great flow of water, the San Juan has twice been known to cease flowing, during the droughts of 1896 and 1934.

The San Juan, the Green, and Colorado rivers are the only rivers of Utah on the list of principal rivers of the United States Geological Survey. They are among the mighty and most mysterious rivers of the world, flowing for much of their length in deep, dark canyons, frothed with fierce rapids, filled with jagged boulders, and altogether forbidding for much of their lengths. Until recent years only a few parties had ever succeeded in traveling very far down their courses.

Other unusual rivers of Utah include the Bear. This is the largest river in the Western Hemisphere that does not reach the ocean. Starting in the Uinta Mountains, the Bear travels 500 miles (804.6 kilometers) to cover only 90 airline miles (144.8 kilometers) and ends in Great Salt Lake. The Virgin River squeezes itself into Virgin Narrow, almost 2,000 feet (609.6 meters) deep and only a few yards wide. When the vehicular tunnel was cut in Zion Canyon, huge boulders were dumped in the valley. The force of the Virgin River water is shown by the fact that in floods even these giant rocks were carried away.

Among other Utah rivers are the Weber, Ogden, Provo, Spanish Fork, Sevier, Yampa, Price, San Rafael, Fremont, Paria, and Kanab. The Escalante River has been called "one of the most spectacular and least-known rivers in the United States."

Although Utah is usually thought of as lacking in water, strangely, only five other states have a greater area of inland water. Until recent years, however, Utah's saline waters have not been very profitable.

The most spectacular lake in Utah and one of the world's most notable bodies of water is Great Salt Lake. The density of salt in the lake runs as high as 25 percent. Only the Dead Sea has greater salt content. The water levels vary greatly, and some experts feel that eventually Great Salt Lake will evaporate entirely. However, it has been known to increase as well as decrease in size. Usually there are sixteen islands in Great Salt Lake, but when the water is low, some of these are connected to the mainland and become peninsulas. Antelope is the largest island in the lake.

Boats on the lake are sometimes endangered by storms and high waves. When a storm hit one scientific party, the leader said, "I had never expected to ride a storm at sea in semi-arid Utah." There is no danger of drowning since nothing sinks, but there is a considerable threat of death by strangulation in the bitter salty water.

The largest freshwater natural lake in Utah is Utah Lake, and its pure waters have long been a blessing to the state. Bear Lake is shared with Idaho. Panguitch and Navajo are other lakes. Artificial lakes include Deer Creek, Pine View, Rockport, Strawberry, Echo, Sevier Bridge, Otter Creek, Piute, and Flaming Gorge. The great

*The American Fork River in winter.*

Glen Canyon Dam itself is in northern Arizona, but most of Lake Powell, created by the dam, is in Utah.

Building this dam was long and bitterly opposed by naturalists and others because it would cover many interesting formations and archaeological sites, but it was finally decided that the need for water, hydro-electric power, and recreation outweighed other considerations.

## MOUNTAINS AND OTHER FEATURES

Most of Utah's life-giving water flows into the valleys from mountains and plateaus. Snow and rains that fall on the highlands come down into the parched lower areas in the form of rivers and streams, springs and underground water.

The most important mountain ranges in Utah are the Wasatch and Uintas. The Uintas are the only major range in the United States running in length from east to west. The highest point in Utah is King's Peak in the Uintas, with an elevation of 13,528 feet (4,123 meters). As recently as 1940 Mt. Timpanogos near Provo, 12,008 feet (3,660 meters) high, was listed as the highest point in Utah.

Other ranges and groups include the Abajo, Promontory, Newfoundland, Cedar, and Beaver mountains. Some Utah mountains are volcanic in origin, including the extinct volcanoes of southern Utah and a volcanic region near Price. Thermal activity underground is still shown in such features as the mineral spring craters called "hot pots" near Heber City, and the hot springs to the north of Salt Lake City.

Included within Utah's borders are some of the true desert and wilderness areas. One explorer said of one of these places that it was "measurably valueless except to hold the world together." The Great Salt Lake Desert was rightfully one of the most terrifying places to travelers in the old West. Today the hard-packed salt there forms the world's best auto racing surface—the Bonneville salt flats. Other extensive deserts are the Sevier and the Green River.

Some of the desert areas, such as Utah's Painted Desert and the Coral Pink Sand Dunes, have great beauty.

Natural features of interest include Mammoth and Timpanogos caves, and Hurricane Cliff which runs near Utah's southwestern

*The San Rafael Swell*

boundary, reaching heights of almost 2,000 feet (609.6 meters). The Raplee Anticline, an upfold of stratified rock near Mexican Hat, is so perfect an example of its type that it is often shown in geography books. Another anticline, the San Rafael Swell, is considered one of the geological wonders of America. This swell is the center of a huge bulge in the earth's crust (anticline). Among the great buttes, Windowblind Peak, which towers about 1,800 feet (550 meters) above the road, is probably the highest free-standing butte in Utah.

## CLIMATE AND TOPOGRAPHY

The higher mountain regions of Utah have short summers and extreme winters. In the regions of the larger cities, the climate is moderate with only a few very hot or very cold days. The valleys of the Virgin and Santa Clara rivers are called "Utah's Dixie." They are warm and dry and have almost a tropical climate.

Precipitation ranges from 30 to 60 inches (76.2 to 152.4 centimeters) in the mountains to that of desert areas with 5 inches (12 centimeters) or less per year. When the rains and snows fail, irrigation is threatened and high winds take a heavy toll in soil erosion.

Utah has the third highest average elevation of all the states, 6,100 feet (1,859 meters), just under that of Colorado and Wyoming.

Utah lies within three great topographic regions: Rocky Mountain, Colorado Plateau, and Great Basin. The Rocky Mountain region has an Alpine character; the plateau features a land of flat-topped mountains, buttes, cliffs, deep canyons, and countless formations, all as colorful as the rainbow.

Most of western Utah is in the Great Basin. This was once a huge bowl-shaped depression also covering much of Nevada. Over the centuries soil washed from the mountains by the rivers has filled it to a depth of thousands of feet. It is a lonely region of valleys and remote north-south ranges.

The coming together of these three mighty regions in Utah makes it one of the most picturesque and scenic areas on earth.

# Footsteps on the Land

## ANASAZI: "THE ANCIENT ONES"

Flames of a great bonfire leaped toward the sky amid the weird chanting of the congregation. Overhead the full moon came and went as clouds scudded by. The sacred fire crept up and curls of smoke blackened part of the pink stone walls. Far overhead those rainbow-colored walls soared in an almost perfect arch, while the dim figures alternately raised their hands toward its heights and then bowed in reverence.

We do not really know that such a scene ever took place at the base of Rainbow Bridge, but the blackened smudges of prehistoric campfires lead authorities to believe that prehistoric peoples lit their sacred fires there and paid awesome tribute to their gods.

What little is known about the very early peoples of Utah is told to us by the things they left behind. Stone weapons and other simple objects are found from a period thought to be about ten thousand years ago. However, it is almost certain that men and women lived in the region much earlier than that.

As time went by, they learned how to make baskets and pottery and came to be known as Basket Makers. Twelve or fifteen hundred years ago the more advanced of these Anasazi, or ancient peoples, learned how to cultivate and raise corn and other crops. They dug pits to store their grain and lined them with adobe bricks. At first the pits were thought to be houses, but the roofs were too low for a person to have been comfortable in them.

Gradually the ancient peoples became more skillful in their building. They put up pressed-earth apartment houses called pueblos, sometimes several stories high. These were enlarged over and over again as the population expanded. Some were in the open air; others were built perched in caves on the sides of great cliffs, so their people are known to us as Cliff Dwellers. No one is certain why they

*Opposite: The Sea Gull Monument, dedicated to Utah's state bird who helped save the first crops and keep the pioneers alive.*

went to the cliffs, but it was probably for protection against enemies.

They improved their skills in basket making and agriculture. The dry air has preserved neatly-fashioned yucca sandals, robes woven of turkey skin strips, and yucca cord still wrapped with rabbit fur or bird skins, which they cleverly wove into blankets and other items.

Over the years the Pueblo peoples reached a high level of civilization. Then suddenly and mysteriously their comfortable and valuable dwellings were abandoned. No one knows why. Possibly the rains failed, and they had no water; perhaps terrible epidemics of disease came; or they may have fled from fierce attackers, leaving their homes to be discovered at a later period, almost as though the original inhabitants had gone out only for the day.

Over much of southern Utah, the remnants of their culture are found. Cliff ruins in Zion, an adobe village near Monticello, a rock fort built one thousand years ago in Nine Mile Canyon near Price, and the pit houses of the northwest—all are typical of the wonderful relics of bygone peoples found in Utah. Nine Mile Canyon has the most northerly examples of cliff-dwelling architecture anywhere.

Among the most fascinating works left to us by the ancient peoples in Utah are the petroglyphs and pictographs still found throughout much of the state on rock walls and caves. Petroglyph is the word for a picture message that has been scratched into the sur-

*Prehistoric ruins in Grand Gulch.*

face; pictograph is the same kind of message simply painted onto the surface. There are many of these drawings. They show crude people, beasts, snakes, and other forms. If they were a kind of picture writing, the key to reading them has never been found. Some authorities feel they may be more like good luck omens, or even prayers created to ask for good luck in hunting or warfare.

Hieroglyphic Gap near Parowan, the wonderful large prehistoric murals of Barrier Canyon, and the drawings of Newspaper Rock in Indian Creek Canyon are good examples of this work. One especially fine pictograph of Newspaper Rock was named by visiting Boy Scouts the "All American Man." It is the balloon-like figure of a person daringly painted in bright red, white, and blue, with red and white stripes.


## LAND OF THE EUTAW AND OTHER INDIANS

Three larger groups of Indians have occupied Utah since the time of European visitors to the area: Paiute, Ute, and Shoshoni (including Gosiute). Each of these groups has several divisions bearing such well-known names as Timpiute, Uinta, Beaver, San Juan, Kaiparowits, Cedar, and Kaibab.

Utah takes its name from the Eutaw (or Yuta). Levi Edgar Young, a student of western history, says this name has many meanings, but most of the groups who talked to him about it claimed the name meant "people who live on the heights" or "high-up Indians."

Life was hard in this region, and much of the time was spent in food gathering. Most of the Indians in Utah were not as warlike as the plains Indians to the east. Nor were they as advanced and well-developed as the more easterly Indians. Some of them had no chief and little organization until the Europeans came. Their most-used articles of clothing were rabbit-skin blankets. They had learned to use almost every shred of any animal they managed to kill. Basketry and basket pottery were important to Indians of the area.

When horses of the Europeans began to come into the country, the Ute, particularly, made good use of them in hunting. The Paiute

*Traditions
are carried
on, as at
Bluff
Indian Days.*

lived in crude thatched tepees, while the Gosiute lived in windbreaks without roofs. They were among the most primitive Indians of America. Jedediah Smith called them "the most miserable of the human race."

T.J. Farnum gave a colorful description of the Gosiute in 1845: "They wear no clothing of any description—eat roots, lizards and snails . . . And when the lizard and snail and wild roots are buried in the snows in winter they . . . dig holes . . . and sleep and fast till the weather permits them to go abroad again for food . . . These poor creatures are hunted in the spring of the year, when weak and helpless . . . are fattened, carried to Santa Fe and sold as slaves."

In southern Utah, reservoirs and canals with wooden gates show that the Indians used irrigation successfully to grow crops.

The Indians of Utah were noted for their honesty, according to Levi Edgar Young. When Bishop Whipple of Minnesota visited them, he asked a chief if his belongings would be safe in his tent while he made a long trip. "Yes," the chief replied, "there is not a white man within a hundred miles" (160.9 kilometers).

About five hundred years ago, shortly before Columbus came to

America, an unusual group of Indians came into the Southwest, and some of them made their home in far southeastern Utah. These were the Navajo. They must have come from a long distance, because they were unlike any of the nearer groups, but where they came from and why they made the long trip may never be known for certain. Their language is similar to the Athapascan Indians of western Canada.

They were warlike and have always been a proud people. At one time, about four thousand of them were exiled from their home-lands by the American government, although a small band in Monument Valley never was forced to surrender. After four years, the exiles were permitted to come home, and eventually the great Navajo reservation was created, with a small part in Utah, south of the Colorado River.


## ON AN OLD SPANISH TRAIL

In 1540 Captain García López de Cárdenas led a party of his fellow Spaniards to the brink of the Grand Canyon of the Colorado River. Just what part they saw or where their exact path led has never been known. Some say they probably touched what is now Utah, but that is now considered very doubtful. At any rate, they very likely saw part of the land of Utah in the distance.

However, they brought back with them such an awful description of the terror and uselessness of the land that the Spanish to the south left it alone for over two hundred years. During that period some Europeans may have been in Utah, but no accurate records have been found.

Not till the year of American independence, 1776, did Europeans of record reach Utah. Catholic Fathers Silvestre Velez de Escalante and Francisco Atanasio Dominguez led a party through the region in a search for a California route and started back. With great hardship they passed through the Virgin River country and discovered Glen Canyon, desperately searching for a place where the mighty Colorado could be crossed. Finally they cut stone steps from the top to the bottom of the gorge and passed over the river and out of Utah.

The place where it was thought they had passed was called Crossing of the Fathers, but later it became known that the real crossing was at the mouth of Padre Creek, about a mile (1.6 kilometers) away.

This expedition was followed by many Spanish caravans trading with the Indians of the Great Basin, and later dealing with settlements in southern California. Eventually the route of these trading parties became known as "The Old Spanish Trail." One branch of this entered Utah south of the La Sal Mountains, passed through present-day Moab, Green River, Castle Valley, Salina Canyon, along the Sevier River Valley nearly to Panguitch, across the plateau to Paragonah, southwest to the Pine Valley Mountains, and then on to southern California by way of a route that is paralleled by today's Highway 91 in some areas. A principal object of these traders was to enslave Utah Indians, and this practice continued until it was outlawed in 1852.

## RENDEZVOUS OF THE FUR TRADERS

By 1819 British fur trappers had come into the region of what is now Utah, closely followed by Americans also after furs. In the winter of 1824-25, Jim Bridger descended Bear River to Great Salt Lake. Although Etienne Provost was the first to sight the lake, Bridger is usually named as the discoverer because he was the first to reach its shores and taste its bitter water. At first he thought it was an arm of the Pacific Ocean. Bridger later told a tall tale of a terrible snowstorm in the region that killed and froze all the buffalo there: "All I had to do was tumble 'em into Salt Lake an' I had pickled buffalo enough for myself and the whole Ute nation for years." Actually, this tragic winter caused the virtual extermination of buffalo in Utah.

The river and town of Provo are named for Etienne Provost, and Ogden takes its name from another extraordinary early trapper-explorer, Peter Skene Ogden.

In 1826 the firm of Smith, Jackson and Sublette was organized to carry on the fur business. Rugged, kindly Jedediah Strong Smith set out to explore the territory with a thoroughness it had never known before. He was one of the great frontiersmen of American history. Crossing through Utah and the Mohave Desert, he became the first person to complete an overland journey from the Missouri River to California. The next spring he forced a passage over the Sierra Nevada, and crossed the wastelands of Nevada and western Utah to his base at Bear Lake. He was the first to cross the Great Basin in both directions, and he knew the Utah country as no other person did in this period.

The expedition of Captain B.L.E. Bonneville missed Utah, although he sent some men of the party through Utah on the way to California.

The first European settlement in Utah was made by Antoine Robidoux, who built several shelters and a fort in the 1830s.

Each year the trappers held what was called the annual "Rendezvous," in Utah or other parts of the West. These were among the most picturesque gatherings ever held in America. In the winter of

*The annual rendezvous.*

1825-26, a large group of trappers settled down in skin tents on the present site of Ogden. When Indians stole eighty of their horses, they made a daring raid into the Indian camp and came back not only with their own horses but with forty more for good measure.

The summer rendezvous at Ogden in 1826 was among the wildest of all. General William H. Ashley came from St. Louis with a caravan of one hundred laden pack animals. There was a carnival atmosphere of games, races, singing, and story telling. The rendezvous were held from 1825 to 1840.

In 1841 the first party of immigrants ever to go overland from the east to California passed through Utah. This was the Bartleson-Bidwell company of thirty-three people. They skirted the northern edge of the Great Salt Lake Desert. With this party was nineteen-year-old Nancy Kelsey, who became the first white woman ever to enter what is now Utah.

Most important to the opening of the Great Basin region were the explorations of Captain John C. Frémont in 1843, 1844, 1845, and 1854. Most of the territory he covered had already been explored by trappers and others, but he brought a scientific background to the task, and his reports were thorough and detailed.

When he saw Great Salt Lake for the first time, Frémont found it "stretching in solitary grandeur far beyond the limit of our vision. It was one of the great points of the exploration, and as we looked eagerly over the lake in the first emotions of excited pleasure, I am doubtful if the followers of Balboa felt more enthusiasm, when . . . they saw for the first time the Great Western Ocean."

Frémont and his men explored much of the lake in a leaky rubber boat. On September 9, 1843, they landed on an island that has since been named for Frémont. Frémont considered himself the first to explore the lake in a boat, but trappers had done this as early as 1826. On a later visit, aided by low water, Frémont splashed across to Antelope Island on horseback and gave it that name. In the expedition of 1845, guided by the scout Kit Carson, Frémont's party made the first crossing by non-Indians of the central Salt Desert. It has been said that "Fremont's report opened the West to the nation's understanding."

*Sunset over the Great Salt Lake.*

Utah's first permanent European settlement came into being in 1844-45 when Miles Goodyear built the first fort west of the Wasatch and called it Fort Buenaventura.

The ill-fated Donner-Reed party took a shortcut and had to hack their way through Wasatch canyons. They rested too long on the present site of Salt Lake City and were caught farther on in the snows of the Sierras. They helped to prepare the trail to Salt Lake for those who were to come later.

By this time the stage was set for the one of the strangest and most remarkable epics in the history of the world.

## THE SAINTS COME MARCHING IN

A group of wagons emerged from Emigration Canyon and paused on a hill overlooking a valley. A man rose in one of the wagons. He had not been well and was still pale, but he retained the look of a leader. His eyes swept the valley before him. He said very little, but the few words he spoke have become among the best-known quotations of history: "This is the place; drive on." The man, of course, was Brigham Young, president of the Church of Jesus Christ of Latter-Day Saints, generally called the Mormon Church.

The day Young arrived at the hill overlooking what was to become Salt Lake City—July 24, 1847—has become an outstanding holiday of the church, called Pioneer Day.

The words of Clara Decker Young, wife of Brigham, are not so well known. She later wrote, "When my husband said, 'This is the place,' I cried, for it seemed to me the most desolate in all the world."

*The wagon train of the Saints entering the*
*Salt Lake Valley from Emigration Canyon.*

Contrary to common belief, Young did not choose the spot for its beauty and natural wealth. It was a desolate-looking place indeed. Earlier Young had said almost with despair, "If there is a place on this earth that nobody else wants, that's the place I am hunting for." When he saw the forbidding land of the Great Salt Lake, he said at once, "This is the place."

Such a decision had been forced on the Mormons by the hostility of people who could not understand their beliefs and "strange" ways. They had been driven from New York; from Kirtland, Ohio; Jackson County, Missouri; and finally were forced to abandon fine homes and their thriving and beautiful city of Nauvoo, Illinois. Their founder and leader, Joseph Smith, and his brother had been killed in Illinois. They desperately wanted a place where they would be the first settlers, where they could say to others, "This is our land!" as had been so often said to them. As early as 1842, Joseph Smith had predicted that his people would someday settle in the Rockies.

In 1846 the Mormons began to move across Iowa. They created the Mormon trail across the territory, established settlements and supply stations, and helped greatly in opening up the western part of Iowa, which became a state in that year. By the winter of 1846 the incredible number of four thousand Mormons went into a camp near what is now Council Bluffs, making almost overnight a new city on the frontier—called Winter Quarters. Five hundred thirty log houses and eighty-three sod houses were built by skilled craftsmen under the energetic direction of Brigham Young. There were city blocks and regular streets.

To Winter Quarters came Jesuit Father P.J. De Smet, who had made a remarkable prediction about the West in thinking about the "unhappy poor" of Europe. "Why are ye not here? Your industry and toil would end your sorrows. Here you might rear a smiling home and reap in plenty the fruit of your toil . . . Broad farms with orchard and vineyard, alive with domestic animals and poultry, will cover these desert plains to provide for thick-coming cities, which will rise as if by enchantment with dome and tower, church and college . . . hospitals and asylums."

At Winter Quarters the Mormons asked Father De Smet "a thousand questions about the . . . valley, which . . . pleased them greatly from the account I gave them of it. Was that what determined them? I would not dare to assert it. But they are there," Father De Smet wrote.

As the Mormons wintered in Iowa, a call came from the United States Army for volunteers to help fight in the war with Mexico. Five hundred young Mormon men called the "Mormon Battalion" enlisted and began a journey overland to San Diego, California. That march, led by Colonel Phillip St. George Cooke, has gone down in history as the longest infantry march on record in the United States. Chaplain David Pettegrew kept a diary of the journey, one of the most interesting in our history. A typical entry reads: "December 25—It is Christmas day. We are without food or water. We have traveled twenty miles (32 kilometers) and camped at night without finding water." The Mexican War was over before they arrived, but they had done much to open up the West. Eventually, much of their route was used by the Southern Pacific Railroad.

The first group of Mormon settlers began to move westward from Winter Quarters on April 7, 1847, to "find an abiding place for the saints." Under Orson Pratt's leadership an advance company entered the valley of Great Salt Lake on July 22, 1847. The very next day they dedicated the land to God, asked Divine blessing on the plantings, began to break ground, dug a ditch from the clear flowing creek, and made a small dam to divert the water. Pratt's journal says, "This afternoon we commenced planting our potatoes after which we turned the water upon them and gave the ground quite a soaking." And so the first acts of the pioneers in Great Salt Lake Valley were to worship, plow the soil, irrigate, and plant.

The next day the main company, led by Brigham Young, pitched their camp on what came to be called City Creek. That first brave party began with 143 men, 3 women, and 2 children. At Fort Laramie another small group joined the party, making a total of 161. The women were Ellen Sanders Kimball, Clara Decker Young, and Harriet Page Wheeler Young; the children, Isaac Perry Decker and Lorenzo S. Young.

Five days after Young's company arrived, the advance group of the Mormon Battalion rejoined their families and friends in the valley of the Great Salt Lake. Altogether about two thousand people had reached Utah by the fall of 1847. During that summer 80 acres (32 hectares) were planted to potatoes, corn, beans, turnips, buckwheat, and other edibles. Fall wheat was planted on about 300 acres (121 hectares). By the spring of 1848, a total of 5,000 acres (2,023 hectares) of wheat and barley had been planted; it grew, and every day as more Saints arrived "their souls were touched with gladness as they looked at the valley which already had been turned to green by their fellows."

Then a "black cloud" appeared on the horizon. Hordes of crickets began to swarm in, devouring every green leaf and stalk as they advanced. A Mormon battalion veteran, John Murdock, said, "Never did I experience such a terrible time as when the crickets swept down upon our fields of grain to destroy them." Elizabeth Dilworth wrote, "A messenger met our company . . . and apprised us of the scourge of crickets . . . and yet we knew that God would deliver us."

The deliverance came in the form of a bird. "Out of the blue" suddenly arrived another horde—snow-white sea gulls from their homes on the islands of Great Salt Lake. They swooped down on the crickets and devoured them ravenously, saving enough of the crops to prevent famine. Ever since that time the story of the gulls has been one of the most popular in western history. With its special place in the hearts of the people, the sea gull has become the state bird.

More and more pioneers continued to stream in; construction increased; the future looked bright, peaceful, and serene. But it was not to be so.

*Many pioneers reached the promised land after hauling what they could in simple two-wheel carts.*

# Yesterday and Today

Almost as soon as he arrived, Brigham Young inspected the area of what is now Salt Lake City and without hesitation located the future site of the temple. The city was planned in great blocks ten acres (4 hectares) square, with very wide streets; a fort was constructed as well as small houses of adobe and logs.

During the first period of Mormon occupation, the region was still considered part of the Mexican lands, until it passed into United States hands after the treaty ending the Mexican War. The first "laws" of Utah were the decrees of Brigham Young. Then in December of 1848, a provisional state of Deseret was established, including present-day Utah, Nevada, and much of Arizona, Idaho, Wyoming, Colorado, New Mexico, and even portions of Oregon.

By 1849 waterpowered sawmills, gristmills, and a carding machine had all been established.

For about two years the Mormons had been almost completely isolated. Now, however, gold-seeking forty-niners were flooding across the plains, taking all routes to what they hoped would be the riches of California. Many of them used the Utah crossings. Parley Pratt wrote to his brother, "After crossing the great prairie wilderness for a thousand miles (1,609 kilometers), where nothing is seen like civilization or cultivation, this spot suddenly bursts upon their astonished vision like a paradise in the midst of the desert."

The coming of the gold seekers meant a great deal to the settlers. The Mormons could trade horses, provisions, and other necessities the forty-niners needed for the prized possessions they were carrying with them. Desperate travelers were willing to sacrifice priceless goods for the necessities of their trip. The surprised Mormons received, at ridiculously low prices, many comforts of life otherwise unavailable. The forty-niners traded these for food, fresh horses, mules or oxen, and other supplies that they needed.

The energy, resourcefulness, and terrible sacrifices with which the devoted Mormons developed Utah and the surrounding areas during the next several years are almost incredible. Bountiful and Farmington came into being in the same year as Salt Lake City. The first

35

permanent white settlement in Utah, on the site of Ogden, was purchased from Miles Goodyear by the Mormons, and they began the development of Ogden in 1848. Provo and Utah Valley were settled in 1849; Manti and Sanpete Valley, 1849-52; Tooele, 1849; Genoa in Nevada, 1850; Nephi and Fillmore, 1851; Brigham City, 1851; San Bernardino in California, Parowan (the first settlement in southern Utah) and Cedar City, all 1851; Santa Clara, 1854; and Las Vegas in Nevada, Morgan, Moab, and Fort Lemhi in Idaho, all were settled in 1855.

Founding and building so many settlements, almost all in inhospitable areas, required a devotion to duty that only could have been found in a deeply religious group. Their success forms a contrast to the failure of most of the communal-type communities being set up elsewhere in about the same period. Only the settlement of the Catholic church in such areas as the coast of California can be compared with the Mormon's accomplishments in their "epic story of hardship, sacrifice, failure, and triumph."

By 1850, the civilization that the Mormons had tried to escape was again creeping up on them. Congress, in that year, created the Territory of Utah. Although many were suspicious of him, Brigham Young was named first territorial governor by President Fillmore. Four territorial officers were not Mormons. In 1852 the town of Fillmore was chartered as the capital because of its more central location. However, this did not work out and the capital was brought back to Salt Lake City.

In 1852 the Church of Jesus Christ of Latter-Day Saints accepted polygyny (usually called polygamy) as part of its official doctrine. They considered that it was a man's religious duty to provide for as many wives as he was able, and very strict rules were established for the well-being of the multiple marriages. However, this practice caused great troubles before many years had passed.


## WALKING ACROSS THE CONTINENT

In 1855, thousands of people were leaving Europe for America because of the Crimean War and high food prices. Many of these were converts to the Mormon religion from Scandinavia and other areas. They came to the end of the Missouri rail lines, but most of them could not afford to buy oxen and carts for the long trip across the continent to Utah.

Governor Young wrote, "They will be provided with handcarts on which to haul their provisions and clothing. We will send experienced men . . . to aid them . . . they are expected to walk and draw their carts across the plains. Sufficient teams will be furnished to haul the aged, infirm and those unable to walk. A few good cows will be sent along to furnish milk and some beef cattle. . . . ''

Singing the song "Some Must Push and Some Must Pull," seven hundred fifty handcart pioneers made the trip within eight months after Young wrote—hauling the simplest kind of two-wheel cart. They were allowed only 17 pounds (7.7 kilograms) of baggage per person, and many prized belongings had to be disposed of.

An early winter overtook two of the handcart parties in 1856; they were stalled by snow, almost completely without food. Rescue parties gathered up supplies contributed by the Mormon people. Some women contributed the clothes off their backs. The rescuers pushed across the snowy wastes to aid the starving handcarters.

When they reached the travelers, one rescuer reports: "The train was strung out for three or four miles (4.8 or 6.4 kilometers). There were old men pulling and tugging at their carts, many of which were loaded with sick wives and children. We saw little children, six and eight years of age, struggling through the snow and mud. As night came on, the mud and snow froze to their clothing."

A member of the party described another scene. "When the handcarts arrived at the bank of a ford, one poor fellow who was greatly worn down with travel, exclaimed: 'Oh dear, I can't go through with that!' His heart sank within him and he burst into tears. But his heroic wife came to his aid, and in a sympathetic tone said: 'Don't cry, Jimmie, I'll pull the handcart for you.' In crossing the river, the shins and limbs of the waders came in contact with sharp cakes of ice, which inflicted wounds on them which did not heal until long after reaching the valley."

Many died on the way; sometimes the survivors had to huddle together against dead bodies for warmth. At last the rescue parties brought the survivors into Salt Lake City, where everyone was taken into the homes of fellow Mormons.

Altogether in the period from 1856 to 1860, four thousand people crossed the plains in handcart companies. One seventy-three-year-old woman walked all the way from Iowa City to Salt Lake City.


## THE PIONEER LIFE

For many their new life would be as full of dangers, hardships, and work as the journey to Utah had been, especially in creating settlements in remote wilderness areas. One of these treks has been called a "western epic."

The church called 256 members to settle the San Juan country. The route was completely unknown. They wandered on, trying to find a place to cross the Colorado River. On Christmas Day, 1879, they "cooked the last of their food. That Christmas dinner was a slapjack of flour and water baked in a frying pan." An advance party made an eleven-day trip to the nearest settlement for more supplies.

Finally they decided to go down the canyon wall through a slit known as "Hole in the Rock." This turned out to be only 10 feet (3 meters) wide in some spots and almost straight down. They had to blast rock away in some places with black powder, and hack footholds in the rock at other places. In going down they had to hook as many as sixteen braces of oxen to the back of each wagon to keep it from crashing down the slope. They had hauled lumber for 60 miles (96.5 kilometers) to build a ferry to cross the river. There were almost unbearable hardships in the remainder of the trip, but six weeks later they arrived to settle such towns as Bluff, Monticello, Mexican Hat, and Blanding.

According to Hoffman Birney, their trip "was labor beside which the toil of the emigrant that crossed the entire continent to California and Oregon was child's play.... Nowhere in the history of America is there a more impressive example of the power of a creed,

38

*Hardy travelers are immortalized in a detail of Pioneer Monument.*

of the faith that moveth mountains, than in the conquest of the Hole in the Rock and the story of the Saints of the San Juan.''

Wherever the wilderness breakers went into desolate new land, they had almost nothing but a few household belongings and oxen. They either went without or made what they needed. A wash basin might be carved in a stump of a cottonwood tree, with a drain hole drilled in the bottom and plugged. The Deseret Agricultural Society gave prizes in 1860 for homemade plows, shovels, washing machines, threshers, steam engines, lathes, harnesses, and even rifles made from crowbars, or ''revolving'' pistols.

Mary Ann Orton, daughter of pioneers, wrote: ''My mother herded sheep, sheared them, washed and carded the wool; then spun it and wove it into cloth. From it she made blankets, shawls and clothing. She dyed the cloth of dyes made of rabbit brush and also the minerals found in the hills. We children gleaned the wheat left in the fields; the heads were taken off, and the straw preserved and made into braids and sewn into hats. The straw was bleached with sulphur found in the mountains.

''Sometimes we made fancy ornaments of straw, particularly for little Xmas [sic] remembrances. . . . We raised sugar beets and made molasses. Many a happy evening was spent during the long winters by pulling candy. Not a bit was wasted. On Christmas Day, if we children could pull some candy, we asked for nothing else."

Bartering was common among the pioneers and is illustrated by the story of ingenious Mrs. M.L. Ensign. She wrote after her husband was sent abroad, "An Indian came to me with a nice buffalo robe, which he wanted to trade . . . for old clothes and a brass kettle. Soon thereafter another Indian traded me a pony for the robe. I sold the pony for a yoke of small oxen and 300 pounds (136 kilograms) of flour. Immigrants came along and traded me a yoke of large oxen, which were very poor, for my oxen, which were fat. The poor oxen soon became fat on our meadows, and I sold them for $110 in cash, thus . . . from a few old clothes and a brass kettle I soon realized $110 in cash and 300 pounds (136 kilograms) of flour."

The cultivated land that is so beautiful today was made that way by toil "almost beyond endurance."

At Manti, rattlesnakes appeared by the hundreds. According to one pioneer, "They crawled everywhere. They attacked the horses and the cattle; they crawled into the bedding; they were found in the dugouts and one of the brethren killed thirty in one day."

Another pioneer wrote, "We toiled hard and lived on a few greens and on thistle and other roots. We had sometimes a little flour and some cheese . . . Some . . . were compelled to go with bare feet for several months, reserving our Indian moccasins for extra occasions."

Some little pleasures and comforts came their way, however. Ox teams hauled a two-thousand-volume library and 2 tons (1.8 metric tons) of school books over the plains to Salt Lake City. A beautiful square piano was brought in by wagon.


## TROUBLES IN PARADISE

In 1855, a plague of grasshoppers caused much more severe damage than the earlier plague of crickets had done.

However, another "plague" was to be even more severe. This was trouble with the Indians. In general, the Mormons dealt much more kindly with the Indians than did other settlers. Brigham Young had said it is "far cheaper to feed and clothe the Indians than to fight them." Nevertheless, when settlers took over the Indian lands, there was bound to be trouble. In 1853 a disturbance called the Walker War began. Walker was one of the more warlike Indian chiefs. Captain J.W. Gunnison and his men were massacred. The settlement at Spring City was destroyed by fire, and the settlers had to keep watch constantly. The situation would have been much worse without the help of the great Ute, Chief Soweitte, who was always friendly to the settlers and counseled peace. In one Indian council Soweitte took a whip to Chief Walker for calling him a coward.

Finally, Governor Young and his aides visited Chief Walker in his camp. When they walked into the chief's tent, he refused to rise, but did shake hands. After a long silence, an old chief rose and spoke: "I am for war. I never will lay down my rifle and tomahawk. Americans have not truth. . . . One year gone, Mormon say, they no more kill Indian. Mormon no tell truth, plenty Utahs gone to Great Spirit — Mormon kill them. No friend to Americans more."

After considerable discussion, Walker said he would give his answer the next day. Young offered sixteen oxen and some trinkets and clothing to the old chief, and the Indians were pleased. Finally they assembled again, and Walker spoke. ". . . when Mormon first came to live on Wakara's land, Wakara gave him welcome. He gave Wakara plenty bread and clothes to cover his wife and children. Wakara no want to fight Mormon; Mormon chief very good man; he bring plenty oxen to Wakara. . . . All Indian say 'No fight Mormon or Americans more.' If Indian kill white man again, Wakara make Indian howl."

The pipe of peace was passed, and Governor Young signed a peace treaty with the Indians.

However, warfare continued off and on with the Indians until the end of the Ute Black Hawk War in 1868. The major Indian troubles were over then. As recently as 1921 there was a small uprising of Paiute led by "Old Posey." This revolt ended when Posey was killed.

"War" of another kind was even more disturbing to the Mormons. Brigham Young had been named in 1854 to a second term as governor of Utah Territory, but opposition was growing. United States judges were hostile to the Mormons, who felt their decisions were biased. Non-Mormons throughout the country were becoming increasingly bitter over polygamy. They helped keep alive a myth that Mormons, not Indians, were responsible for the Gunnison massacre. Many other clashes occurred.

Judge George P. Stiles returned to Washington from Utah and reported that the Mormons were in a state of rebellion. President Buchanan removed Brigham Young as governor and appointed Alfred Cumming to succeed him. On July 24, 1857, just ten years after the pioneers first reached Utah, the Mormons were celebrating that anniversary and the remarkable accomplishments of a mere ten years when news was brought that the United States Army had entered Utah. The great distance between Washington D.C. and Utah made accurate and up-to-date communication difficult.

General Albert Sidney Johnston had been ordered to put down the Mormon "rebellion." Brigham Young said they did not want war, but they would fight the United States if necessary. He issued a "proclamation" forbidding U.S. troops to enter Utah. When they came anyway, the people of Utah decided to move on, remembering their troubles in Missouri and Illinois. In a strange episode, more than thirty thousand people evacuated their homes and cities. Governor Cumming reported: "The roads are everywhere filled with wagons loaded with provisions and household furniture, the women and children often without shoes or hats, driving their flocks they know not where.

"They seem not only resigned but cheerful. 'It is the will of the Lord,' and they rejoice to exchange the comforts of home for the trials of the wilderness. . . . Young, Kimball and most of the influential men have left their commodious mansions, without apparent regret. . . . The masses everywhere announce to me that the torch will be applied to every house . . . so soon as the troops attempt to cross the mountains. I shall follow these people and try to rally them."

President Buchanan sent Colonel Thomas L. Kane, a friend of the Mormons, to act as mediator. He finally worked out a settlement, and the people returned to their homes. The army marched through Salt Lake City in a friendly manner and built Camp Floyd about 45 miles (72 kilometers) away. Cumming continued as governor in name, while Brigham Young carried on most of the functions of civil government as president of the Mormon church.

The troops stayed in Utah until the beginning of the Civil War in 1861. President Lincoln wondered about the loyalties of Utah. Brigham Young telegraphed, "Utah has not seceded but is firm for the Constitution and laws of our once happy country."

## PERSECUTION

In 1862, again doubtful of Utah's loyalty, the government sent Colonel Patrick Edward Connor and three hundred toops to Utah, and Congress passed a law aimed at polygamy. At first, Connor was violently anti-Mormon. He was also cruelly anti-Indian. At the Battle of Bear River, he ordered all the Indians killed without mercy.

As time went on, anti-Mormon views were shared by more and more of the people of the United States, who especially hated polygamy. Several more laws were passed against it. Contrary to general opinion, the vast majority of Mormons were not polygamists, but hundreds of those Mormons who did have more than one wife were disfranchised and imprisoned for practicing polygamy. Many fled into hiding and exile.

Finally the corporation of the Church of Jesus Christ of Latter-Day Saints was dissolved and its property confiscated by the national government. Large numbers of non-Mormons were coming to Utah, and friction between the groups increased.

Over the years non-Mormons, called "Gentiles" by the Mormons, had accused the Mormons of many crimes. Among these was the terrible Mountain Meadows Massacre in 1857, when one hundred travelers were killed in southwestern Utah. Long after the event, John D. Lee was convicted and executed as a leader in the plot that led those unarmed people to be slaughtered. Only two children survived the massacre. They were sent by Brigham Young to relatives in Arkansas.

Brigham Young died in 1877, and his successors had an extremely difficult time.

Finally, in 1890, the president of the Mormon church at that time, William Woodruff, issued a manifesto advising Mormons to give up polygamy. Soon after this decision, polygamists were pardoned, their civil rights restored, and church property returned.


## A MODERN STATE

On several occasions, Young and other leaders attempted to have Utah admitted as a state. They formed a government for the non-existent state of Deseret, and the legislature of this "ghost government" met for nine sessions in the hope that Congress would create the new state.

The present boundaries of Utah had been fixed as early as 1868, and Utah was far more ready for statehood than many states that had been admitted earlier, but the suspicions of Congress and the people were too strong concerning the Mormons. It was not until January 4, 1896, that Utah at last became the forty-fifth state of the United States.

As the twentieth century came to Utah, the first gasoline automobile bumped over the roads from Ogden to Salt Lake City. One hundred ninety-nine were killed in an explosion of the Winter Quarters mine at Schofield. In 1903, railroad passengers and freight began to go directly across an arm of Great Salt Lake on a marvelous new trestle completed in that year. This was called the Lucin Cutoff. A bridge of another kind (and another color) made the news in 1909 when Rainbow Bridge was discovered by Dean Byron Cummings.

When World War I seared Europe, the thrift of the Mormons was put to good advantage. Every season when it was possible, Mormon Relief Societies saved grain to be used in case of crop failures. The wheat from these granaries was sent overseas to save the children of

France from starvation. Twenty-one thousand Utah men served their country in the war, and 760 died in service.

During the twenties and thirties, the Nazi party grew in power in Germany. For their symbol of hatred, the Nazis had borrowed the age-old symbol of friendship of the Navajo Indians—the Swastika. In 1940, sadly, the loyal Navajo banned their symbol that had taken on a meaning so far removed from friendship.

In World War II, 70,000 of Utah's men and women took their places in the armed services. Two thousand four hundred died in this war.

In the decades of 1960 and 1970 there was unprecedented growth in Utah's economy. However, one of the most important energy projects of the country, the Kaiparowits power project in southern Utah, a plan to use Utah's enormous coal supplies, was defeated in 1976 after years of controversy with environmentalists.

The Mormon church rapidly expanded as it pushed forward with its worldwide missionary movement and built as its world headquarters the magnificent new skyscraper building, not far from Temple Square. A new visitors' center was built and a multi-million-dollar arts center was designed to provide for the famous Utah Symphony Orchestra and other arts programs that make the city a center of culture of a vast area.

## THE MORMON CONTRIBUTIONS

From gold rush days to the present, non-Mormons have been moving into Utah. Mining leadership was largely non-Mormon, and these Utahans have achieved success in Utah banking, merchandising, and other businesses. Mormons and non-Mormons worked to achieve statehood. Utah's Japanese, blacks, Greek, Italian, German, Jewish, and Mexican people are all proud of their state's heritage, and all are a part of it.

However, Utah today is still a Mormon state in many ways. Two thirds of its people are members of the Church of Jesus Christ of Latter-Day Saints. Utah is the worldwide headquarters of the Mor-

*The Mormon Tabernacle Choir*

mon religion, which is rapidly growing in many other lands. Mormon pioneer culture, architecture, monuments, religious characteristics, and colonizing practices "have placed an indelible imprint on the state that is immediately apparent to visitors." Many place names are taken directly from the *Book of Mormon:* Nephi, Manti, Moroni, Lehi, and Deseret.

Even today's visitors are apt to be "struck with wonder," as Levi Edgar Young once pointed out, "at the immense results produced in so short a time by a handful of individuals." Part of their success is due to the application they give to a task. They do not accept smoking or drinking of alcohol, tea, or coffee; they are taught to give 10 percent of their income and often more to the work of the church, and many Mormon youths hope to be "called" for two years of missionary work to build their church's membership. In addition, the Mormons have been "practical and far-seeing social planners."

As a consequence, perhaps never before in human history has such devotion, intelligence, and hard work been "applied to the problem of converting wilderness into lush productive land."

They built great cities and erected incredible temples, but they left an inheritance of more than physical things. The Tabernacle Choir was established by Brigham Young in the 1850s, and probably no musical organization is better known or more respected around the world today. Drama and music were presented for more than sixty years at the old Salt Lake Theater, opened in 1862. Today a replica, Pioneer Memorial Theater, offers modern facilities for drama. Most of the church units have outstanding choirs and choruses and drama groups and sponsor frequent dances. The arts center is one of the most advanced of its kind.

Although they were considered by some to be stern and forbidding, the early Mormon people loved to sing and dance. Several flat rocks along the pioneer trails are known as "Dance Rock," where the tired travelers still found enough energy to break out the fiddle and have a rollicking time.

Like other states, Utah today is a complex society with representation of every religion and race. That this diversity can exist together in such a wholesome way is a tribute to the ability of people to get along together.

Altogether, it must be said that Utah and its people have achieved a unique position in the heroic saga of the winning of the West and modern-day living of quality and depth.

*Aspen trees have replaced firs that were cut down during the mining period. Their leaves turn golden in the autumn.*

# Natural Treasures

## ANIMALS, PLANTS

If you should come upon a small black and white animal standing motionless on his front paws, with his hind paws in the air and his tail waving about like a palm frond, you will know you have just encountered Utah's little spotted skunk. He seems to find it fun to stand on his head. Give him a wide berth; he is a straight-shooter for more than 10 feet (3 meters), and his scent is the strongest of the skunks.

One of Utah's unique animals is the pika or rock rabbit. This creature was not even known until 1905. It has a peculiar bleating cry unlike any other.

Among the larger animals, some of the biggest deer herds in the nation are found in the plateau country. Elk, Rocky Mountain sheep, pronghorn antelope, and mountain lion or cougar roam the wilds. Antelope Island boasts one of the few herds of wild buffalo remaining in the United States. At one time Utah had an entirely different kind of grizzly bear than has ever been seen alive.

Of the fur bearers, the beaver has made a comeback, and in the Uinta Mountains the prized marten is second only to beaver.

Utah claims that "no hunter needs to go away disappointed." Hundreds of thousands of mule deer have been bagged, a total that probably places Utah at the top of deer-hunting states. Chinese pheasants, quail, mourning doves, and Hungarian and chuker partridge are ranking game birds of the state.

Among other birds, visitors are usually surprised at the number of "ocean" birds. Great flocks of sea gulls thrive. Even more surprising are the hordes of pelicans such as the colony on Bird Island. Although they must fly 100 miles (160.9 kilometers) for food, they always return to their protected paradise. Whistling swan and wild turkey are among Utah's rarer birds. The water ouzel, which swims with its wings, is an interesting member of the bird population. One of the largest refuges in the United States is the Bear River Migratory Bird Refuge. Another is Fish Springs Migratory Bird Refuge.

About the only life that can survive the thick brine of Great Salt Lake is the almost transparent little brine shrimp. However, trout, perch, catfish, and other game fish all delight the angler in the many freshwater lakes and streams.

In spite of the vast arid reaches, there is forest land in each of Utah's counties. Only about 3,000,000 acres (1,214,058 hectares) of forest are commercial. Blue spruce, the state tree, Engelman spruce, gnarled and twisted Siberian junipers, ponderosa and lodge pole pine, and Douglas and Alpine fir are all found. Ponderosa is the most important commercial tree. The limber pine has been called "eccentric." Dwarf maple and scrub oak add flaming reds to autumn's colors, as does the quaking aspen its bright yellow. Aspen is America's most widely distributed tree. Utah has the largest aspen known.

The most important tree to the early Indian was piñon pine. The tiny nut provided much of their food. Sticky gum surrounding the pine cone provided a waterproofing compound. Among the most interesting of Utah trees is the bristlecone pine. Some of these trees in other areas are now considered to be the oldest living things in the world. The cottonwoods of Utah's streams have long provided valuable and welcome shade and wood. The Aquarius Plateau has one of the highest evergreen forests in the world.

There are between three and four thousand species of plants growing in the Aquarius Plateau. The best known is the sage—called "the hallmark of the American desert." Mark Twain observed about the sage, "As a vegetable it is a distinguished failure." Creosote and mesquite also fall into that category. Utah canyons are spectacular with wild flowers in the spring, and the large snow-white columbines are especially showy. Desert cactus also puts on a great display of bloom. An exotic flower is the datura, a creamy night blossom of Zion Canyon, resembling a morning glory, with an exotic perfume.

The bulb of the state flower, the Sego lily, was eaten boiled or ground into flour. Chewing gum was contrived from milkweed juices, and even the lowly cattails found a place in cushions and mattresses. Joshua trees were named by Mormon pioneers, who thought they held their arms to the sky like Joshua in prayer. Actually they are not trees but a member of the lily family.

50

*Pronghorn antelope*

## "TREASURE HOUSE OF THE NATION"

Levi Edgar Young predicted that "Utah will someday be the treasure house of the nation." Two hundred ten useful minerals are found there. Great Salt Lake may prove to be a great source of future mineral wealth in addition to its salt.

Iron Mountain west of Cedar City is one of the world's richest hematite deposits. Utah salt reserves could supply the world for a thousand years. There is enough coal to fill the world's needs for over two hundred years. Ninety-two billion tons (83,461,000,000 metric tons) of oil shale, carbon dioxide, helium, natural gas and oil, asphalt, semi-precious stones such as jet, agate, chalcedony, jasper, garnet, opal, obsdian, olivimite, rock crystal, and topaz are all found.

Ozokerite is a kind of mineral found only in Utah and Austria. It provides one of the most perfect insulators known. Gilsonite is another rare carboniferous mineral available in Utah.

In Utah, however, water is perhaps the most precious mineral of them all. Unfortunately, it probably will never be plentiful, but steps have been taken to preserve and protect the available supplies.

# People Use Their Treasures

## MINING AND METALLURGY

The smelting industry began in Utah in 1910. Today minerals bring about a billion dollars into Utah annually. The "father of Utah mining" was Colonel Patrick E. Connor. The Mormons deliberately avoided the wealth of minerals, but Colonel Connor encouraged the "Gentiles" to find and use the minerals because he thought it would help to break the Mormon hold on the country.

The most spectacular mining activity in Utah today is in copper. From the yawning man-made canyon of the open-pit Utah Copper Mine of Kennecott Copper Company at Bingham comes more than 99 percent of Utah's present copper production. This one mine produces about one fifth of all United States copper. The tremendous mineral deposits of Bingham Canyon were discovered by the Bingham brothers in 1850. Altogether, Utah ranks second among the copper producing states of the country. It is also second in silver and third in lead and gold production.

Silver mining provided some of the most uproarious mining days in Utah history. Famous mine names in Utah silver include the Horn at Frisco (the richest silver producer in Utah), the Emma, and Silver Reef. A British group bought the old Emma for five million dollars. Almost immediately the ore petered out. The scandal of this so-called fraud even involved President Grant, but it was proved that the owners sold in good faith and did not know the ore was gone. Silver Reef at one time turned out grindstones. When these were found to be full of silver, the grindstone business was quickly discontinued. Now many of the famous silver towns are ghosts.

The mineral gilsonite was discovered by and named for Sameul H. Gilson, a man who had once been a Pony Express rider. His wife reported, "I'll never forget the day he brought the substance home. Then began a series of experiments ... every place I turned there was some of the sticky stuff. He made chewing gum, paint, insula-

*Opposite: A Union Pacific Railroad poster for May 10, 1869.*

53

*The copper mine at Bingham.*

tion . . . '' This gleaming brittle type of asphalt is particularly valuable for insulation, since it will not burn. Millions of tons are found in the Uinta Basin, the only known commercial source in the world.

Oil was discovered at Virgin in 1903 and at Mexican Hat in 1907, but major oil production did not begin until the 1950s. The current annual production of petroleum is better than forty million barrels, mostly taken from southeastern Utah.

Old Iron Town west of Cedar City smelted the first iron made west of the Mississippi. Today, Utah's rich iron ore deposits have helped make Provo the most important steel center in the West. Limestone and dolomite mined at Payson are used in iron smelting. Utah is also the number-one coal producing state west of the Mississippi, although the high figure of 1929 is a far cry from current production. Coal mining is centered at Price.

Today, potash is produced by a huge mining complex near Moab. This area is also rich in uranium ores.

One valuable mineral is not found in Utah, although at one time a lot of people thought it was. Two prospectors claimed to have found diamonds by the sackful at Diamond Gulch near Vernal. Mining engineers visited the site and predicted large diamond mining activities. However, it was found that the prospectors had ''salted'' the mine with diamonds from South Africa. This was one of the largest swindles of its kind in American history.

## MANUFACTURING AND AGRICULTURE

Manufacturing in Utah began with the home industries of the pioneers. By 1850 a woolen mill and a pottery plant were in commercial operation. The first foundry used the scrap iron left by immigrants along the trail. This crude beginning has been succeeded by such mammoth operations as the Geneva Steel Works, near Orem in the Provo region, one of the largest in the world of its type.

Brigham Young ordered sugar machinery from France to use the sugar beets his people were growing. For a long time the effort was not successful, and only molasses resulted. Finally, a chemist discovered that the soil of France in which the beets were successfully grown was acid, and the Utah soil was alkaline. Other chemicals had to be added to create sugar in the crystalline form. The first successful beet-sugar plant began operating at Lehi in 1890, and this has been an important industry in the state since that time.

Today Utah's products range from those of the world's largest Swiss cheese plant near Logan to solid rocket fuels for the first stage of missiles made by Thiokol Chemical Company at Brigham City. In total, value added by manufacturing in Utah now stands well over a billion dollars per year.

Movie making has been one of the more colorful industries of Utah. The scenic wonders of the state, especially in the southern part, have provided background for many motion pictures, including such well-known titles as *Drums Along the Mohawk, Thunderhead, My Friend Flicka, Wagon Master,* and *Stagecoach.* Popular television series such as *Wagon Train, Have Gun, Will Travel,* and *Death Valley Days* have been filmed in Utah.

Most of Utah's crops are grown on irrigated acres. Utah Mormons pioneered in rules for the use of water. When a group of Mormons found their irrigated land had become too alkaline to grow crops, in desperation they planted grain in the dry, unirrigated land. They were amazed to harvest a crop, and from that time on "dry farming" has been a constant practice. As late as the 1880s, however, David Broadhead was indicted for perjury in court because he said that crops could be grown in the region without irrigation.

As early as 1851 the Mormons raised cotton. By 1866, at Brigham Young's order, a cotton mill came into operation near St. George.

Today, hay amounts to almost half of the total value of all crops grown in Utah. In order of value, other crops are wheat, sugar beets, alfalfa seed, potatoes, and barley. The state is noted for its wonderful fruits. Cherries, apples, peaches, apricots, and such famous melons as the Greenriver watermelon and cantaloupe are grown with irrigation.

Livestock accounts for the largest part of farm income in Utah. About 80 percent of the land of the state is used for grazing. Animals find good forage even on the high plateaus in summer, but descend to lower levels for the winter.

The total value of agricultural products in Utah is about a third of a billion dollars per year. At one time the largest share of Utah income came from agriculture. Then mining took its place. Since World War II, manufacturing has been the greatest revenue producer.

## TRANSPORTATION AND COMMUNICATION

One of the most far-reaching events in American history took place in Utah in 1869. Until then, transcontinental travelers had been forced to take the long, hard, dangerous, dusty way across the continent by foot, or horseback, or by wagon. The stagecoach was faster and more comfortable, but the fare was three hundred fifty dollars from St. Joseph, Missouri, to Salt Lake City.

By 1868, picturesque track crews were laying rails across Utah with unbelievable speed—spurred on by offers of bonuses. The Union Pacific Railroad was building toward the west from Omaha. The Central Pacific was hurrying toward the east to meet it—no one knew just where.

At last, on May 10, 1869, after seven years of work, beset by Indian attacks and every other hazard, the East and West were ready to be joined at Promontory, Utah. Sidney Dillon, first president of the Union Pacific, described the scene: "At a little before eleven o'clock the Chinese laborers began levelling up the roadbed, preparatory to placing the last ties in position ... Governor Leland Stanford of California and party arrived ... There were cheers for everybody from the President of the United States to the day laborers ... The two engines moved nearer to each other ... The two superintendents of construction ... placed the last tie ... of California laurel highly polished, with a silver plate in the center bearing an inscription."

A number of ceremonial spikes had been donated by the various states along the route; the most important were two gold spikes from California. Holes had been drilled in the polished tie to take the spikes easily. Finally the gold spikes were put in the holes; a telegraph operator attached wires to one so that striking the spikes would activate special telegraph keys in every major U.S. city and announce the joining of the country. Governor Stanford stepped up, grasped the silver sledge hammer and took a mighty swing—and missed the spike completely! However, the telegraph operator covered the confusion by pressing the key, and the word went across the land.

The mighty deed was done. The first trains began to roll the next day. An English traveler, Isabella Bird, passed over the rails a few years later and described the trip through Utah: "Soon after sunrise we were running down the Great Salt Lake, bounded by the white Wasatch ranges. Along its shores, by means of irrigation, Mormon industry has compelled the ground to yield fine crops; we passed several cabins, from which even at that early hour Mormons, each with two or three wives, were going forth to their day's work ... At Ogden we changed cars, and again traversed dusty plains, white and glaring, varied by muddy streams, and rough arid valleys, now and then narrowing into canyons.

"By common consent the windows were kept closed to exclude the fine white alkaline dust ... The wheel marks of the trail to Utah often ran parallel with the track, and bones of oxen were bleaching in the sun, the remains of those whose carcasses fell in the wilderness on the long and drouthy journey."

*Thomas Hill's famous painting,* Driving the Last Spike.

On January 10, 1870, a branch road was completed to Salt Lake City. This branch was the first railroad west of the Missouri River built entirely without governmental subsidy. A company headed by Brigham Young completed the road largely with materials grown or made in Utah.

The first law passed in Utah provided for the proper care of roads and bridges. The Mormons coined a phrase—"dugway"—to describe their deep-rut roads, where wagons, sunk almost to the hubs, could go slowly around the slopes of very steep mountains. The Salt Desert highway was built in 1925 and required an entirely new principle of highway construction. Today's highways are modern in every respect and generally follow trails made by Indians, trappers and traders, and Mormons.

Even in arid Utah, water transportation has played a part. In 1871, a stern-wheel steamboat was operating on Great Salt Lake carrying machinery and ore. Later it became an excursion boat and finally ended up as a boat house at Garfield Beach.

Communication in early Utah was sketchy. When travelers met on the prairies they would exchange letters to be carried back by those going in the opposite direction. It was a great day when the speedy Pony Express first arrived at Salt Lake City—April 7, 1860. The fee was as much as five dollars per letter, but worth every cent because of the dangers and great expense of the operation.

The Pony Express was not to last long, because the overland telegraph was completed to Utah in 1861. At last the isolated region could communicate with the rest of the country at the speed of electricity.

Today's mail, as well as passengers and freight, comes not with the speed of light but almost with the speed of sound. The airport at Salt Lake City is one of the country's great and important air terminals.

The first newspaper in Utah was the *Deseret News,* established June 15, 1850, at Salt Lake City. When supplies of paper ran low, the publisher appealed to his readers to contribute old rags from which paper could be made to keep his newspaper going. Subscribers often had to pay for their subscriptions by barter.

Today, the Mormon church owns one of the state's two largest

*On a trip through Grand Gulch in southern Utah, tourists can see many, large well-preserved Anasazi Indian dwellings.*

daily newspapers, publishes some of the most important magazines of Utah, and operates a large printing plant. A television station, the mountainous West's first radio station, and a shortwave broadcasting facility are also owned by the Mormon church.

Modern Utah "communicates" in another way with over nine million tourists every year, who come to marvel at the state's wonders and who contribute hundreds of millions of dollars to the Utah economy.

60

# Human Treasures

## LEADER OF THE SAINTS

It has been predicted that Brigham Young will someday be recognized as the most brilliant genius in the development of the American West. Certainly he is "one of the major figures in western history, a man of enormous energy and vision."

He was born at Whitingham, Vermont, in 1801. At the age of thirty-one he joined Joseph Smith in western New York and became a charter member of the Quorum of Twelve of the Mormon Church in 1835. On the death of Smith, Young became the leader of the church.

The list of plans he made, the projects he conceived, the businesses he conducted, the twenty-seven wives he married, the decisions he reached, the people he assisted, and his almost ceaseless activity—all help to give a picture of an incredible human being.

Most important of all was his "amazing genius as a colonizer." In the thirty years between 1847 and 1877, Brigham Young founded or planned three hundred fifty Mormon colonies. Probably no other one man can equal that colonizing record. In many of the colonies, such as Salt Lake City, he took a continuing and leading part. To all of them he gave personal attention and regular consideration.

The personality of this amazing man is revealed to later generations through his writings. Following are a number of random quotations that may provide insight into his personality:

On conditions in Utah, 1850—"On the twelfth of May, peach trees of two years' growth were in bloom . . . But on the 7th of June . . . a severe frost . . . which injured the vines and tender plants. Yet we feel confident that this valley will yet produce the choicest fruits, as it does now the richest vegetables . . . Our State House is enclosed . . . several departments will be ready for . . . the General-Assembly; the High School rooms; the printing office, and tithing, post and recording office—the coming winter . . . Preparations are made for the establishment of a Parent School for qualifying teachers . . . for enclosing the university lands; and for everything else which may tend to facilitate the improvement of the old and the young alike in the knowledge of the arts and sciences, and general intelligence."

Philosophy of government—"Legislation should ... not be bound down by contracted and selfish views, old and exploded policy or traditional errors. Let a spirit of freedom and liberality pervade all our acts, and an enlightened and highly practical course of legislation will surely be the result ... Be it our aim to direct our political affairs so as to promote union, integrity, and independence to the territory, industry, knowledge, and truth to the people. Thus shall we secure to ourselves peace and freedom, and transmit to our people those free institutions which we received as a free legacy from our forefathers."

Concerning education—"It is very desirable that the Saints should improve every opportunity of securing at least a copy of every valuable treatise on education—every book, map, chart, or diagram that may contain interesting, useful and attractive matter, to gain the attention of children, and cause them to love to learn to read; and also every historical, mathematical, philosophical, geographical, geological, astronomical, scientific, practical and all other variety of useful and interesting writings, maps, etc., ... for the benefit of the rising generation."

On the first Thanksgiving in Utah—" I recommended to all the good citizens of Utah that ... they rise early in the morning ... and wash their bodies with pure water; that all men attend to their flocks and herds with carefulness; and see that no creature in their charge be hungry, thirsty or cold; while the women are preparing the best of food for their households, and their children ready to receive it in cleanliness and with cheerfulness ... I further request that when the day has been spent in doing good, that you end the day ... with praise and thanksgiving, and songs of rejoicing. Retire to your beds early and rise early again and continue doing good."

The first letter sent from Salt Lake City, August 4, 1847—"We have delegated our beloved brother Ezra T. Benson and escort to communicate to you by express the cheering intelligence that we have arrived in the most beautiful valley of the Great Salt Lake, that every soul who left Winter Quarters with us is alive and almost

62

*A portrait of Brigham Young.*

everyone enjoying good health ... Let all the brethren and sisters cheer up their hearts and know assuredly that God has heard and answered their prayers and ours, and led us to a goodly land, and our souls are satisfied therewith.''

During the thirty years he spent in Utah it is likely that Brigham Young remained ''satisfied'' almost until the day he died, August 29, 1877, with the land that he was so much responsible for developing.

One researcher on Young comments, ''I know of no instance where he acted unreasonably, or unfairly, or impractically.''

## CONQUEROR OF THE WILD RIVERS

The first party to conquer the lower Green River and the unknown and mysterious canyons of the Colorado was led by a one-armed army major, one of the most unusual of the many intrepid explorers who blazed the way in Utah.

This was John Wesley Powell, who began his trip near the present-day town of Green River, Wyoming, with a nine-man crew in four boats and enough supplies for a year.

One boat was lost in Lodore Canyon, and continuing difficulties plagued the party. Major Powell was a hard man to get along with, and he and his men had many arguments. Three men deserted the group, "fed up" with the whole thing. When they reached the plateau above the river, they were killed by a group of Indians who probably refused to believe that they could have come from the riverbed below.

Major Powell kept careful notes, and his book about the trip, *Exploration of the Colorado River of the West,* has become one of the classics of its type. Following is one of his colorful descriptions: ". . . a strange, weird, grand region. The landscape, everywhere away from the river, is of rock; crags of rock—ten thousand strangely carved forms—rocks everywhere, and no vegetation, no soil, no sand . . . a whole land of naked rock, with giant forms carved on it; cathedral shaped buttes, towering hundreds or thousands of feet; cliffs that cannot be scaled, and canyon walls that shrink the river into insignificance, with vast, hollow domes, and tall pinnacles . . . all highly colored—buff, gray, red, brown, and chocolate; never lichened; never moss-covered, but bare, and often polished."

In one canyon, Major Powell almost lost his life, but the party finally came through to the Grand Canyon of the Colorado on August 30, 1869, and made their way 300 miles (483 kilometers) northeast to Salt Lake City.

Major Powell helped to solve the mysteries of the Colorado in his thrilling journey. Lake Powell, which was created by Glen Canyon Dam, was named in his honor.


## OTHER CREATIVE PEOPLE

Utah was the birthplace of the "Western" story. The writer Zane

Grey had been living in Utah, becoming acquainted with cowboys, heroes, and villains of the West, learning about roundups and roping, branding, riding, good times, and hardships of the cow country. Grey lived at Kanab when he began to put all these experiences down in a book, which he called *Riders of the Purple Sage*. This book formed the pattern for most of the many Western books written by Zane Grey. It has also been the pattern for most of the great flood of Western books, movies, and television shows that have delighted not only this country but the world. Another of Zane Grey's books is *Wildfire,* the story of a Utah horse.

A prominent Utah author, known best for her poetry, is Phyllis McGinley. Bernard De Voto, an Ogden native, is ranked among the best-known of Utah's writers.

Probably the most noted artist born in Utah was the sculptor Mahonri Young, a grandson of Brigham Young. Mahonri Young was invited to create a monument in memory of the sea gulls that saved Mormon crops. The result was the beautiful, graceful Sea Gull Monument in the Temple grounds at Salt Lake City. The four plaques on this monument have been called "among the best reliefs in America." He began his art career as a painter, and his *The Blacksmiths* hangs in the state capitol. Possibly the best-known work of Mahonri Young is the mammoth granite and bronze *This Is the Place* monument, erected at the mouth of Emigration Canyon in 1947 to commemorate the centennial of the pioneers.

Cyrus E. Dallin, born in Springville, is another prominent Utah sculptor. His Indian statues are much copied. They include *The Appeal to the Great Spirit* and *The Medicine Man.*

The photographic record of the West created by C.R. Savage includes many pictures considered classics in photography. He set up his studio at Salt Lake City in 1860. With equipment sometimes weighing 200 pounds (90.7 kilograms), he traveled about the region and has given us a priceless pictorial account of the times. He made the famous photograph of the meeting of the Central Pacific and Union Pacific trains at the driving of the golden spike ceremony, and this has been reproduced in almost every school history and history of railroading.

*Frontiersmen with muzzle loaders.*

## SUCH INTERESTING PEOPLE

Utah has contributed a number of outstanding inventors. Those who like television will probably consider Philo T. Farnsworth one of the great benefactors of mankind. Farnsworth, born at Beaver, is usually said to be the most important single person in the development of television. He developed the picture tube and can probably be considered the father of modern television. He demonstrated an earlier system of television in 1927 when he was only twenty-one years old.

Browning has long been an important name in the history of firearms. The Brownings, John M. and Jonathan, of Ogden, are noted for their inventions and improvements in automatic weapons.

66

Dr. Harvey Fletcher, born in Provo, has been called the "patron saint" of the hard of hearing. He invented the audiophone and other instruments to help the deaf hear better. He also invented the audiometer, to measure hearing ability. An "inventor" of another kind was John Henry Seely, who has improved the famed Rambouillet breed of rams.

A number of prominent Indian leaders have made their homes in Utah. Levi Edgar Young called Kanosh, chief of the Pahvants, "one of the noblest Indians that ever lived." Another chief, Washakie, was described by a pioneer as "a great and good chief, and helped many companies of emigrants on their way to Utah. He always was our friend, and when he came to the city we made him and his followers welcome, and whenever he left he gave his assurance that 'Washakie and men would always love Mormon pioneers.'"

One of the most notable friends of the Indians was Jacob Hamblin, a leader in the settlement of southern Utah. He traveled on some occasions with Major J.W. Powell, who wrote of Hamblin, "He is a silent, reserved man, and when he speaks it is in a slow, quiet way, that inspires great awe. His talk is so low that they must listen attentively to hear, and they sit around him in death-like silence. When he finishes a measured sentence, the chief repeats it, and they all give a solemn grunt."

The nine rules for dealing with the Indians developed by Jacob Hamblin are remarkable guides for human behavior.

Among interesting Utah people is Tom Spalding, entomologist. He was the first to discover the *Philotes spaldingi* butterfly, and altogether twelve kinds of butterflies have been named in his honor. Buck Lee was a prominent leather carver, but he is possibly better known as one of the finest tellers of "tall tales."

Utah has produced many educators of national stature.

Among prominent Utah men in government service, Ezra Taft Benson served as secretary of agriculture in the cabinet of President Dwight D. Eisenhower. He was long an official of the Mormon church. Mrs. Ivy Baker Priest served as treasurer of the United States. Former Governor George H. Dern was secretary of war under Franklin D. Roosevelt.

# Teaching and Learning

The University of Utah claims to be the oldest state university west of the Missouri River. Only three years after arriving at Salt Lake Valley, the Mormons were thinking about a university. But the university was begun in 1850 as University of Deseret. Due to lack of funds it was discontinued in 1855, then revived in 1867. In 1892 the name was changed to the University of Utah.

In about 1875, three distinguished centers of education came into being in Utah. Brigham Young University is in Provo. Salt Lake Collegiate Institute (a Presbyterian school later called Westminster College), and St. Mary's Academy, Catholic, are both at Salt Lake City.

Brigham Young University was established as a Mormon school by Brigham Young. It is usually considered to be one of the world's largest church-related institutions of learning.

Utah State University, Logan, was founded in 1888 as Utah State Agricultural College. It still specializes in the agricultural and engineering education of the region.

Other state-supported colleges are Weber State College, Ogden; Southern Utah State College, Cedar City; College of Eastern Utah, Price; Dixie State College, St. George; and Snow College, Ephraim. The number of college students in Utah in proportion to the population is the highest of any state.

The Intermountain School at Brigham City enrolls several thousand Navajo students. It was founded in 1949, and is operated by the United States government.

Miss Mary Jane Dilworth was Utah's first school teacher. She taught in wagons crossing the plains. Upon arriving in what is now Salt Lake City, she was provided with a "school tent." From there she moved into a lean-to, and eventually a log cabin school was built. Salt Lake City has named one of its modern elementary schools the Dilworth School in her honor.

In the winter of 1851-52 one of the earliest Utah schools met in a log cabin, with George A. Smith as teacher. Evening meetings and

*Opposite: The University of Utah*

*Weber State College in Ogden.*

sessions at the school were lighted by blazing pine knots. Men, women, and children attended.

True to the importance given education in the early days, today Utah spends a greater proportion of its state and local income on education than any other state.

# Enchantment of Utah

Sightseeing in Utah can only be said to be spectacular! The man-made tourist attractions reflect some of the strangest and most unusual activities of our history. Natural wonders are so varied and unique that most of them are duplicated nowhere else, and in no other area of similar size are there so many of nature's marvels.

The federal government has recognized the unique concentration of attractions in Utah by creating twenty-three national preserves of various types within the state. Only California has more National Parks and National Monuments than Utah. However, many other Utah attractions could qualify, and much of the rest of Utah is scenic or notable enough to call for special attention and preservation.

## CITY OF THE SAINTS

Salt Lake City has been called "a living monument to the invincibility of the human spirit." To establish it required a trek across a wilderness and the transformation of a purplish-gray desert waste, covered with sage and sprinkled with only a few cottonwoods.

Most important in the early transformation of that wilderness were the waters of City Creek. Visitors to the city today are delighted to find that instead of hiding the creek in an underground pipe, the city has paid tribute to the watercourse by letting it run swiftly down the street in specially constructed gutters. This valiant little stream still sparkles and gurgles on its way as thousands of feet step across its tiny width each day.

Now the imposing, neat city is renowned as the world center of Mormonism, with international Church of the Latter-Day Saints headquarters housed in an attractive twenty-five-story church administration building.

On his first survey of the future city site, Brigham Young chose the location for many of the landmarks that were later built on the exact places he selected. The plan of the city is impressive. Its blocks are 10 acres (4 hectares) square and its streets 132 feet (40 meters) wide. Authorities have labeled it one of the most beautiful and best-planned cities in the United States.

The heart of the city is Temple Square, dominated by the great towers of the temple, symbolic world center of Mormonism. Only six years after they came, the Mormons broke ground for this structure—in 1853. Forty years were required to complete it. Native Utah granite was hauled by ox teams from Little Cottonwood Canyon to form the 16-foot (4.8-meter) thick walls. The tallest of its six graceful spires is topped with a gleaming gold-leaf-covered statue of the Angel Moroni. Only Mormons are permitted inside the temple itself.

The public is admitted to the nearby world-famous Tabernacle, begun in 1864. It was designed by Brigham Young, and built by Henry Grow, a bridge builder. Grow used principles of bridge building to erect the roof, spanning an area 250 by 150 feet (76.2 by 45.7 meters). The whole thing was put together originally with wooden beams, fastened with leather thongs and wooden pins, because of the scarcity of nails. It seats eight thousand and has acoustics noted all over the world. Visitors are always shown how the dropping of a common pin can be heard the length of the building. Leopold Stokowski complained about the acoustics and said they were not suitable for symphony orchestras. However, the Tabernacle was purposely designed to enhance the spoken word and choral music.

The Tabernacle is home to the world-famous choir, accompanied on the fabulous organ. When it was originally built, the organ pipes were glued with adhesive made from boiled buffalo and cattle hides. Many of the more than seven thousand original pipes are still in use.

One of the oldest houses in Utah, built in 1847, was brought to Temple Square and placed under a decorative canopy. One of the earliest inhabitants of this house, Captain Howard Stansbury, said that "every time it stormed it admitted so much water as called into requisition all the pans and buckets in the establishment."

Temple Square Museum preserves many items of early days, including locks of hair of Joseph Smith and Brigham Young and many articles of their clothing.

Appearing to soar into the air above Temple Square is the world's only known monument to a bird. Soaring Sea Gull Monument is top-

*The great temple in Temple Square*

ped with sculptured likenesses of two of Utah's state birds who helped to save the first crops and keep the pioneers from starvation.

Adjacent to Temple Square is the block containing the former residences and office of Brigham Young. His property was entered by the famed Eagle Gate, now spanning North State Street. The many-gabled Lion House is now a Brigham Young museum, including pictures of twenty-one of his wives and forty-seven of his children. Visitors have often been known to count the gables, believing that each gable represented the apartment of a different wife of the Mor-

*Brigham Young Monument*

mon leader. He never told how many wives he had, but various encyclopedias list the number as at least twenty-seven. Young's nearby Beehive House has been restored. The heroic bronze statue of Young dominates the adjacent intersection. His grave is in a semi-private cemetery.

Utah's impressive capitol building was begun in 1912 and completed in the record time of three years. It is noted for its huge murals and a 3-ton (2.7-metric-ton) chandelier hanging on a 3.5-ton (3.2-metric-ton) chain. The building displays Rockwell Kent's picture *Dennis.* This was donated to the state because Kent, who was scheduled to lecture in Salt Lake City on the "last day" of November, forgot that November "hath thirty days." Kent arrived on the "thirty-first day" of November. To make up for keeping an audience (which never did see him) waiting for hours, Kent donated the picture to the state. A rose garden in front of the capitol is dominated by the great statue of Massachusetts Chief Massasoit.

Pioneer Monument State Park is the site of the huge granite and bronze memorial at the mouth of Emigration Canyon, near where Brigham Young made his famous declaration "This is the place."

The Utah State Fair and International Peace Gardens are both noted attractions of the city, as is the Museum of Daughters of the Utah Pioneers, with its relics of the past. Pioneer Village Museum is a "living restoration of pioneer Utah." The old downtown library has been converted into the Hansen Planetarium.

A twenty-million-dollar civic center occupies 10 acres (4 hectares) just east of Washington Square, the center of territorial and state government until 1915 when the city and county of Salt Lake purchased the building with its romantic memories. The library there is claimed to be among the most modern in America. Offices of public officials and a jail are also included in the center.

Just southwest of Temple Square a twenty-million-dollar civic auditorium and convention center has been constructed. The various auditoriums for music and drama provide one of the finest complexes of this kind in the world.

Salt Lake City's annual "Days of '47" features one of the nation's three largest annual parades. The city's yearly song festival gathers five thousand singers from all over the world.

The 480-acre (194-hectare) campus of the University of Utah has many attractions for visitors, including three museums—the Utah Museum of Natural History, Geology Museum, and Utah Museum of Fine Arts.


## NORTH AND NORTHWEST

A sea serpent is about the last thing anyone would expect in far inland, arid Utah. Yet the monster of Bear Lake has gotten some fine notices. Early Shoshoni Indians claimed that a huge beast inhabited the lake, but that it went away after the heavy winter of 1830 killed the buffalo. In 1868, the *Deseret News* reported "reliable" testimony that S.M. Johnson of South Eden had seen the head of a great animal rearing above the water. Next day four people sighted something that "swam much faster than a horse could run on land." A Mr. Slight wrote that he "distinctly saw the sides of a very large animal that he would suppose to be not less than ninety feet (27 meters) in length ... All agreed that it swam with a speed almost incredible." Whether the monster of Bear Lake was fact or fiction has never been determined.

The highway from Bear Lake to Logan leads through one of America's most attractive glens—Logan Canyon. At the city of Logan is one of the remarkable Mormon temples, built with such devotion and self-sacrifice. A Mormon tabernacle at Logan seats two thousand people.

At Promontory, the federal government has established Golden Spike National Historical Site. Here each year there is a ceremony re-enacting the original Golden Spike ceremony.

When Brigham Young made the last public address before his death in 1877, the town at which he spoke was renamed Brigham City in his honor. The city has boomed in the years since Thiokol Chemical Company began to make rocket fuels there. The Mormon tabernacle at Brigham City is one of the most interesting buildings in Utah from architectural and photographic standpoints. Steam railroading is honored in the Railroad Village Museum there. A wildlife sanctuary of near-record size is the Bear River Migratory Bird Refuge not far from Brigham City.

For many years Corinne was a center for anti-Mormon sentiment. When the citizens of Corinne sent a petition to Congress asking for help, they said Corinne was "the only place where a truly American community can be brought into permanent and successful contact with the Mormon population, whose feet have trodden and who hold in their relentless grasp, every other valley in Utah." As was true of most of Corinne's efforts, nothing ever came of the petition.

The oldest community in Utah, Ogden, was founded by Miles Goodyear, but was laid out by that omnipresent builder Brigham Young. Two unusual museums are of particular interest in this community that has become the second largest in the state. These are the John M. Browning Armory and Firearms Museum and the Relic Hall of the Daughters of Utah Pioneers. The Miles Goodyear cabin is the oldest European structure remaining in Utah.

At the far western boundary of the state lies Wendover, a kind of Jekyll and Hyde city. Half is in Nevada, where gambling is wide

76

open, and the other half is in conservative Utah. Wendover is the supply center and headquarters for activities of a kind that can be held nowhere else in the world. This is the racing in which cars of every type roar across the almost perfectly smooth, rock-hard salt bed of ancient Lake Bonneville. The Bonneville Speedway is known throughout the world, and world land-speed records have been continually broken there.

Little is left of the once flourishing community of Ioseppa, a word which means Joseph in the Hawaiian language, but its story is fascinating. About fifty Hawaiian converts to Mormonism came

*The Bonneville Speedway*

from Hawaii to live there in 1889. The church built a school, chapel, and houses for them. They created a transplanted bit of Hawaii on the Utah desert, but the settlers were almost overcome by leprosy. When a Mormon temple was built in Hawaii, most of the surviving Hawaiian settlers returned to their homeland.


## SOUTHWEST

Much of western Utah is a land of sagebrush and juniper wastes, punctuated by island-like mountain ranges. However, the far southwest has been made to bloom by the ever-present Mormon energy. Washington County is known as Utah's Dixie, where the first settlers were sent by the church to grow cotton.

The founding of St. George was an epic of suffering and endurance, but soon the pioneers were able to erect one of the most distinctive buildings in the country—the gleaming white Mormon Temple of St. George. It can hardly be surpassed as a monument to pioneer effort.

St. George Temple, the first one completed in the state, was built on a bog that had to be filled with more than 17,000 tons (15,422 metric tons) of rock from nearby quarries. At St. George is the old tithing house where Mormon settlers of the region brought every tenth egg or ear of corn, or a tenth of whatever they had earned.

The home of Jacob Hamblin, famous Mormon frontiersman and missionary, has been preserved at St. George, as has the winter home of Brigham Young there.

Nearby Dixie State Park is known for its Snow Canyon, where streams of lava from ancient volcanoes hardened into a formation looking like a waterfall. The Pine Valley church is said to be the oldest chapel still in use in Utah. Pine Valley is proud of its record of being the first community of the state to report in elections.

The ghost town of Silver Reef brings memories of beloved Father Lawrence Scanlon, who was offered the use of the Mormon Tabernacle for his Catholic services. However, there was no Catholic choir, and the Mormon choir volunteered, although of course they had never sung a Catholic mass. In two weeks time, the Mormons had learned the music, and the "Gloria" and "Hosanna" rang out in the tabernacle.

Kanab has long been a favored location for filming of Western movies and television. Cedar City is the largest city and the "commercial capital" of southern Utah. Its "colorful" Mormon chapel was built with stones of the brightest reds, purples, and other colors, gathered from many parts of Utah and southern Arizona. Even passing motorists dropped off loads of multi-colored rocks as they went by, to help the church.

Parowan, founded in 1851, was the first permanent settlement in southern Utah. Three miles (4.8 kilometers) away is Vermilion Canyon, a deeply colored canyon of spectacular beauty.

This canyon is on the road to Cedar Breaks National Monument. Cedar Breaks is a vast amphitheater, almost a half mile (.8 kilometer) deep and 2 miles (3.2 kilometers) from rim to rim. The Indians named this spot "circle of painted cliffs," an appropriate name because the bright colors laid bare by erosion are the most spectacular feature of the area.

However, naturally, the dominant natural wonder of the whole southwest region is breathtaking Zion National Park, given national park stature in 1919. It is one of the most spectacular areas anywhere and of course it is unique in all the world.

Zion is the wonderland carved by the powerful Virgin River North Fork. It is the river that helps the green foliage to grow all along the canyon bottom, making such tremendous contrast with the colors of Zion. These colors, vivid and unbelievable, have a range through every shade from red at the bottom to white, pink, and gold at the top.

One of the most rewarding times to see Zion is at night during the full moon. The colors appear in strong moonlight, with a very unearthly effect. Probably the best-known single feature of Zion is the Great White Throne, a gigantic column of rock 2,500 feet (762 meters) high.

The Zion Narrows of the Virgin River are so narrow that even in daylight stars overhead can be seen by those looking up at the thin

*The Great Arch of Pine Creek Canyon in Zion National Park.*

slot of sky. The Kolob Canyons are eight lesser ravines cut into the plateau. If possible, their colors are even more brilliant than the main canyon.

Zion was discovered by Joseph Black, a pioneer Mormon homesteader. His poetic descriptions appeared so exaggerated that those who had not seen it laughingly called the canyon "Joseph's Glory." When it became clear that Black had not exaggerated the beauties, they called it Zion. Brigham Young is reported to have objected to giving a heavenly name to an earthly place, so they called it "Not Zion," but the original name was restored later.

## CENTRAL: HEART OF UTAH

The picturesque Indian name for Bryce Canyon means "bowl-shaped canyon, filled with red rocks standing up like men." Others have called the flaming spectacle "a sunburst of beauty."

Not so romantic was old Ebenezer Bryce, for whom the canyon was named. He was the first settler in the canyon, in 1875, and in his opinion it was only "a terrible place to lose a cow."

An Indian legend of the origin of Bryce says that the Indians of the god Coyote were working there to make a city, but the Indians took so long with their work that the great god was displeased; he turned them to stone and in his wrath threw over them the bright paints they had been about to use to paint their buildings. There they have stood in colorful stone formations ever since.

Bryce Canyon was made a National Park by Herbert Hoover in 1928. It is entered at the rim, and there are trails to the floor. As the trails are descended from top to bottom, the visitor is able to trace fifty million years of geological history in the carved walls of the canyon. These have been eroded over eons of time by wind, rain, snow, and frost.

Rim Road at Bryce has been labeled the "most colorful twenty miles (32 kilometers) in the world," as mile after mile the wonders of nature's masterpiece of erosion and color are revealed.

Geographically, Bryce marks the dividing line between the Colorado River region and the Great Basin region.

Nearby Grosvenor Arch, south of Cannonville, is considered one of the most beautiful of all natural formations. Another natural formation that gained fame in an entirely different way is the chocolate and yellow hill that was the inspiration for the folk song "Big Rock Candy Mountain," the unique name the peak still bears.

Kimberly, one of Utah's most beautifully situated but least-known ghost towns, has had a varied career of boom, death, and resurrection. Today little remains to testify of its days of vibrant activity except some huge waste deposits and a few crumbled or crumbling buildings. The town of Annabella bases its claim to fame on "the best cold drinking water in the world."

Richfield city park is built on the site of an old Indian village, and in front of the Mormon chapel there is the old treaty tree under which the treaty was signed ending the Ute Black Hawk War.

Fillmore was once the capital of Utah, selected by Brigham Young because of its central location. The fine old capitol building is now a fascinating pioneer museum.

A humorous newspaper article once reported: "The Sunday closing law is so strictly enforced in Salina, Utah, that the busy editor of the Salina *Sun* had to go to church to get the town council together and secure a permit to accept one dollar on a subscription that one of his readers had traveled two days to give him. It was only after explaining that it would cost one dollar and fifty cents to keep the subscriber over, thereby putting himself fifty cents in the hole, that the august body, the council, consented to allow the subscriber to deposit the dollar in a hole by a fence post so that Howard could secure it when the midnight hour struck that night. Howard stood guard over that fencepost like a good 'Injun.' However, he caught a cold that it cost him three dollars and eleven cents to buy mineral water and lime juice to cure."

Towering over Manti in its setting of green lawns and verdant trees is another monument to Mormon determination and ability—the million-dollar cream-colored limestone temple completed there in 1888.

Mount Nebo Scenic Loop near Payson has been described as "one of the most beautiful and exciting drives in Utah." Dating from pre-Civil War days, Old Stagecoach Inn at Fairfield is now the center of a state park.

Provo, named for Etienne Provost, trapper and explorer, is today the West's leading steel center. At Brigham Young University, Provo visitors will see an excellent group of botanical, geological, archaeological, and fine arts collections, plus the Summerhays Planetarium.

Provo Peak Loop Road, Provo Canyon, and Utah Lake are scenic attractions. An aerial tramway lifts viewers to the top of Bridal Veil Falls in Provo Canyon. To the Mormon pioneers Utah Lake was the "Sea of Galilee" in their new "Holy Land." The river connecting

*The North Peak of Mt. Timpanogos.*

Utah Lake with Great Salt Lake they called the Jordan in honor of the river in Palestine connecting Galilee with its own great salt lake—the Dead Sea. Of course, the rivers flow in different directions of the compass.

For a long time Mt. Timpanogos was considered the highest peak in Utah. Its Timpanogos Cave National Monument is one of the finest of the smaller caves. It features filigree of pink and white transluscent crystals.

Alta was once a rip-roaring mining camp. One hundred ten killings are said to have taken place in a single one of its many saloons. At one time a mysterious stranger appeared in Alta and offered to resurrect the dead. Within a short time the people of the town had taken up a collection to persuade the stranger to leave town. Apparently they were not too anxious to have most of the dead brought back to life among them.

Brighton, just south of Alta, was also a rip-roaring town. Today

*Skiing in Alta.*

both these towns are ski resorts. They have strong competition from Utah's splendid Snowbird resort and its aerial tram, and from Park City, an old mining town, booming again. Hotels, restaurants, and "melodrama" theater have sprung up over the old Park City mine shafts. The big attraction is Treasure Mountain, a complex of ski runs, chair lifts, and tow bars.

An aerial tramway lifts gondolas, seating four, to the top of Treasure Mountain, where there is a restaurant. Passengers may ride several miles across the mountain on a mining train. They may leave the train to be lifted over 3,000 feet (914 meters) in a bucket lift. Golfing, horseback riding, and other activities take over in warmer weather. As many as ten thousand people from Salt Lake City and elsewhere may be found on the Park City ski slopes on a winter Saturday.

One of Utah's greatest tourist attractions is a man-made canyon, the huge open Bingham pit gouged out of the face of the earth in search of the low-grade copper ores that supply such a large part of America's supply of that metal. The surrounding land is fast disappearing as the electric shovels, towering three stories tall, gulp the soil. Massive trucks are replacing railroads at the mine.

## NORTHEAST

Red Canyon Overlook affords a grand panorama of the Uinta Mountains, of Flaming Gorge and the Green River, 1,500 feet (457 meters) below. Flaming Gorge Dam creates a lake extending far into nearby Wyoming. Fishing is allowed here 365 days a year.

In 1861, President Abraham Lincoln set aside much of the Uinta Basin for the Indians, where many remained until 1929 when the Kanosh Reservation was established.

Today much of the Uinta region has been set aside as one of the nation's few remaining primitive areas. Highline Trail over the Uintas offers the hardy walker an outstanding hiking opportunity. Brown's Hole and neighboring Robbers Roost in the Uinta Basin have added a great deal to America's lore of western outlaws.

*A peaceful scene in the Unita Mountains.*

Dinosaur National Monument is shared by Colorado and Utah. The unique visitors' center has been built around some of the finest fossils exactly as they were uncovered where they lay on the face of the earth. Authorities constantly come to study these marvels.

At nearby Vernal a replica of an enormous 76-foot (23-meter) dinosaur, Dippy the Diplodocus, constantly enthralls visitors to the Fieldhouse of Natural History.

Skyline Drive, between Tucker and Mayfield, is one of the highest automobile roads in the United States.

## SOUTHEAST: GOBLINS, DRUIDS, ANGELS

Land of Curiosities and Wonders would be a good description of southeastern Utah.

Cathedral Valley is a marvelous scenic area, containing immense rock counterparts of man-made cathedrals, looming up from the sandy floor of the valley.

Capitol Reef National Monument takes its name from the domes of white sandstone that make the region look like the capital city of the desert. The reef itself is a sandstone cliff extending for 20 miles (32 kilometers) across the desert; it rises to a height of more than 1,000 feet (305 meters) above the desert floor.

The town of Escalante was named for Father Silvestre Velez de Escalante, the pioneer European explorer in the area. The town rests at the edge of the vast unpopulated Colorado River Plateau, one of the country's last remaining large unsettled areas. The Petrified Forest and Escalante Canyon are nearby attractions. The village of Boulder has been called the last packhorse town in the country. Until 1935, all supplies had to be carried to the village by pack animal over 36 miles (58 kilometers) of trail from Escalante.

Rainbow Bridge is universally recognized as one of the great natural marvels of the world, the largest natural bridge yet discovered anywhere. It is not accessible by highway or automobile. Some people visit Rainbow Bridge by helicopter.

Although a single small natural bridge in other areas will attract great attention, there are so many of them in southeastern Utah that some scarcely are noticed, and it is thought that many still remain to be put on the maps. Natural Bridges National Monument preserves three huge natural stone bridges—Sipapu, Kachina, and Owachomo. This is a "fantastically eroded" area. Cliff dwellings may also be seen in the region.

No fewer than eighty-eight arches are to be found in Arches National Monument, established in 1929. This outdoor museum demonstrates the structure of the earth and the power of erosion.

Another area made weird and beautiful by erosion is the Upper Grand Canyon of the Colorado, above the junction of the Colorado and Green rivers. This 3,000-foot (914.4-meter) chasm is said by some to be the most spectacular canyon in Utah and in some ways a rival of the Lower Grand Canyon.

Much of the region around the junction of the two rivers has been included in Canyonlands National Park. One of the most fantastic formations of the area is Druid Arch. Its name comes from the resemblance to ancient Stonehenge in England. Druid Arch is formed of two huge sandstone chunks standing upright. Across these stone towers lies a horizontal piece, from which a part of the arch has been carved. That such a monstrous work can be fashioned by wind and rain and frost seems almost too much to believe.

Also included in the Canyonlands National Park are such unbelievable arch formations as Angel, Castle, Fortress, Elephant Trunk, Caterpillar, and Cleft. Many cliff dwelling ruins are also found in the region.

Another national preserve in southeastern Utah is Hovenweep Ruin Canyon Cluster National Monument. This is shared with Colorado and gained national status in 1923. Many well-preserved apartment houses of large size are found in Hovenweep. They have not been occupied for six hundred years or more. The structures are as high as three stories, supported by rafters of cedar logs. Among the preserved ruins of ancient peoples there are several towers of particular interest to archaeologists. No one is quite sure what the peculiar towers were for, and guesses range from grain elevators to lookout towers.

In secluded Goblin Valley the visitor walks through a strange world of carved rock figures in chocolate color. The imagination enables almost every known figure to take shape in the jumbled mass of eroded statuary. One area looks like a ghastly ballroom with distorted figures dancing. The eerie quality of the place, especially as the sun lengthens the shadows of the strange forms, is almost unmatched.

The towering escarpment of Book Cliffs extends in an almost unbroken wall for nearly 200 miles (322 kilometers). The wild country of the magnificent Needles is a maze of pointed rocks, circled with multicolored bands; some of them are topped with strange, squatty boulders so precariously balanced that they appear ready to blow off in the next mild wind, and yet they probably have held their place for centuries.

To the far southeast is the land of the Navajo. In addition to their independent spirit, they are noted for their hand-wrought silver jewelry, sand paintings, and rug making. In every Navajo rug there is at least one small break in the pattern. This is to permit the evil spirit to escape. Like many who refuse to walk under ladders, the Navajo have a similar superstition. They will not walk under a natural bridge in their great outdoor wonderland until they say a prayer.

The greatest scenic attraction of the widespread Navajo country is Monument Valley. Some of these obelisks tower 1,000 feet (305 meters) above the valley floor. There is a quietness almost as of a graveyard—a graveyard dotted with enormous orange and red tombstones. Nowhere on earth are there formations quite like these.

Not many people ever see the only spot in the United States where four state corners come together. One man was asked why he had chosen to spend most of his life in such a desolate region. He said that he was "so close to the four corners that no sheriff could catch him."

The real answer, of course, was that he loved this strange and beautiful region, a feeling that most of the people of Utah, Mormon and non-Mormon alike, share for their unique, industrious, and far-sighted state.

# Handy Reference Section

**Instant Facts**

Became the 45th state, January 4, 1896
Capital—Salt Lake City, founded 1847
Nickname—The Beehive State
State motto—*Industry*
State symbol—Beehive
State bird—Sea gull
State tree—Blue spruce
State flower—Sego lily
State gem—Topaz
State song—"Utah, We Love Thee"
Area—84,916 square miles (219,932 square kilometers)
Rank in area—11th
Greatest length (north to south)—345 miles (555 kilometers)
Greatest width (east to west)—275 miles (443 kilometers)
Geographic center—3 miles (4.8 kilometers) north of Manti
Highest point—13,528 feet (4,123 meters), Kings Peak in Uinta Mountains
Lowest point—2,000 feet (610 meters), Beaverdam Creek, Utah-Arizona border
Mean elevation—6,100 feet (1,859 meters)
Number of counties—29
Population—1,461,037 (1980 census)
Rank in population—36th
Population density—17 persons per square mile (7 persons per square kilometer), 1980 census
Rank in density—42nd
Population center—Salt Lake County, 14.5 miles (23 kilometers) southeast of Salt Lake City
Birthrate—24.2 per 1,000
Infant mortality rate—12.9 per 1,000 births
Physicians per 100,000—151

| Principal cities—Salt Lake City | 163,033 (1980 census) |
|---|---|
| Provo | 73,907 |
| Ogden | 64,407 |
| Orem | 52,399 |
| Bountiful | 32,877 |
| Logan | 26,844 |
| Murray | 25,750 |

## You Have a Date with History

1540—Cardenas may have sighted Utah
1776—Fathers Escalante and Dominguez explore
1813—Infrequent use of "Old Spanish Trail," Santa Fe to Moat to Los Angeles
1819—Canadian fur trappers arrive
1824—Jim Bridger reaches Great Salt Lake
1825—First trappers' rendezvous, Henry's Fork of Green River
1826—Jedediah Smith first crosses Utah
1841—First immigrant party crosses Utah
1843—First of Fremont's explorations
1844-1846—Miles Goodyear establishes first permanent settlement
1847—First Mormon pioneers found Great Salt Lake City
1848—Gulls help save crops
1849—Forty-Niners break Mormon isolation
1850—Congress creates Utah Territory
1852—Plural marriage becomes official Mormon doctrine
1853—Salt Lake City Temple ground broken
1858—End of "Utah War"
1861—Overland telegraph completed
1862—Congress passes anti-polygamy law
1865—Ute Black Hawk War begins
1869—Transcontinental railroad joined in Utah
1877—Brigham Young dies at Salt Lake City
1887—Sterner anti-polygamy law passed
1890—Mormons abandon doctrine of polygamy
1896—Statehood
1903—Lucin railroad cutoff completed
1909—Rainbow Bridge discovered
1919—Zion Natonal Park established
1928—Bryce Canyon National Park established
1947—Centennial celebration
1960—International airport opened at Salt Lake City
1962—Flaming Gorge Dam topped out
1963—Lake Powell begins to form behind Glen Canyon Dam
1964—Canyonlands National Park established; population of Utah reaches a
　　　million
1985—Chief spiritual leader of the Mormons, Spencer W. Kimball, dies and is
　　　succeeded by Ezra Taft Benson; Great Salt Lake rises two feet eight inches,
　　　causing fear of devastation in the Salt Lake City area

*An aerial view of the capitol.*

## Thinkers, Doers, Fighters

Benson, Ezra Taft
Bridger, James
Browning, John
Browning, Jonathan
Dallin, Cyrus E.
De Voto, Bernard
Fletcher, Harvey
Grey, Zane
Kanosh (Chief)
McGinley, Phyllis

Powell, John Wesley
Savage, C.R.
Seely, John Henry
Smith, Joseph
Soweitte (Chief)
Spalding, Tom
Washakie (Chief)
Young, Brigham*
Young, Mahonri

*Utah's representative in Statuary Hall of the Capitol, Washington, D.C.*

## Governors

Heber M. Wells 1896-1905
John C. Cutler 1905-1909
William Spry 1909-1917
Simon Bamberger 1917-1921
Charles R. Mabey 1921-1925
George H. Dern 1925-1933
Henry H. Blood 1933-1941

Herbert B. Maw 1941-1949
J. Bracken Lee 1949-1957
George Dewey Clyde 1957-1965
Calvin L. Rampton 1965-1977
Scott M. Matheson 1977-1985
Wayne Bangerter 1985-

# Index

95

## PICTURE CREDITS

## ABOUT THE AUTHOR

With the publication of his first book for school use when he was twenty, **Allan Carpenter** began a career as an author that has spanned more than 135 books. After teaching in the public schools of Des Moines, Mr. Carpenter began his career as an educational publisher at the age of twenty-one when he founded the magazine *Teachers Digest.* In the field of educational periodicals, he was responsible for many innovations. During his many years in publishing, he has perfected a highly organized approach to handling large volumes of factual material: after extensive traveling and having collected all possible materials, he systematically reviews and organizes everything. From his apartment high in Chicago's John Hancock Building, Allan recalls, "My collection and assimilation of materials on the states and countries began before the publication of my first book." Allan is the founder of Carpenter Publishing House and of Infordata International, Inc., publishers of *Issues in Education* and *Index to U. S. Government Periodicals.* When he is not writing or traveling, his principal avocation is music. He has been the principal bassist of many symphonies, and he managed the country's leading non-professional symphony for twenty-five years.

96